Contents

Sat Nav hints, tips and safety advice
Sat Nav friendly postcodes for places
   Tourist attractions
   Airports and ferry terminals   xviii-xix
   Park & Rides   xix-xxii
   National and Forest Parks   xxii-xxiii
   Out of town shopping centres   xxiii
Motorway network map   2
Mapping of Britain   3-45
Index to place names   46-58

D0238474

Key to map pages

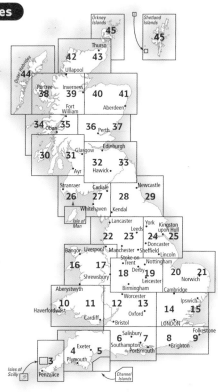

Published by Collins
An imprint of HarperCollins Publishers
77-85 Fulham Palace Road, Hammersmith, London W6 8JB

www.harpercollins.co.uk

Copyright © HarperCollins Publishers Ltd 2009

Collins® is a registered trademark of HarperCollins Publishers Limited

Mapping generated from Collins Bartholomew digital databases

The grid on this map is the National Grid taken from the Ordnance Survey map
with the permission of the Controller of Her Majesty's Stationery Office.

The contents of this publication are believed correct at the time of printing.
Nevertheless, the publisher can accept no responsibility for errors or omissions,
changes in the detail given, or for any expense or loss thereby caused.

The representation of a road, track or footpath is no evidence of a right of way.

Printed in China by Leo Paper Products Ltd.

ISBN 978 0 00 731607 6   Imp 001

WC12447   CUDA

e-mail: roadcheck@harpercollins.co.uk

The basics - how does Sat Nav work?

Satellite Navigation systems use a network of Global Positioning Satellites (GPS) which orbit the earth in known positions. A Sat Nav system receives and compares signals from several satellites to locate the position of the Sat Nav unit on the surface of the earth. You can plan a route to a particular destination by entering its town's name, postcode, address or geographical coordinates. The Sat Nav system works out your route based on whether you've asked for the quickest or shortest route, or whether you've asked to avoid motorways or toll roads etc. Your route is then displayed on a map or as a list of instructions and you're ready to go. If you take a wrong turn or have to divert from the planned route then the device will recalculate the route to get you back on track.

GPS Navigation system

Photo © Daniel Padavona
Used under licence from Shutterstock.com

Choosing a Sat Nav

There are a bewildering number of Sat Nav devices on the market and it can be tough to sort out which one is right for you. Here are some important things to consider when buying your first, or choosing your next, Sat Nav.

- Screen size, clarity and brightness. Larger screens and widescreens are clearer and make using the touch screen easier.

- Portability. You'll need to remove the device from the car when not in use so is it small enough and light enough to fit in your pocket or bag?

- Mounting system. The device needs to be held securely and yet be easy to remove when not in use.

- Map coverage. Do you need maps of the UK, Europe or the whole world? If you regularly take your car to the continent it may well be useful upgrading to Europe-wide mapping.

- Accuracy and date of maps. By the time you get the Sat Nav home the map stored on it could be a year or more out of date. Are you able to download a free update? How much does it cost to download regular updates? – you'd be surprised how much change there is from month to month. Some devices allow you to feed map corrections back to the suppliers so other people can download them to their devices.

- Route planning options. Most devices allow you to choose between shortest or quickest route options but there are other factors you may wish to consider. Can interim points be incorporated into a planned route? Are road names and numbers included in voice directions?

- Internal memory: the larger the internal memory the faster your Sat Nav will calculate, and re-calculate, your route.

- Length of warranty.

- The inclusion of additional features such as Bluetooth hands free communication or MP3 players.

- Real time traffic updates. Many devices have the capability to download up-to-the-minute traffic information so you can be warned in advance of congestion ahead and you can be re-routed to avoid the queues! These services are usually operated on a subscription service so find out how much it will cost per year and how often you're likely to need this service before signing up.

Tips on using your Sat Nav in rural areas

Many of the well-publicised 'Sat Nav nightmares' occur in rural areas, with vehicles ending up stranded on narrow tracks or washed away trying to ford swollen streams. This is often because the maps on which the Sat Nav relies generally don't distinguish between different grades of minor country road. So when it directs you to turn off the main road onto a cunning short cut, it may have no idea whether this short cut is a wide 2-lane road, a single track lane or an un-surfaced track which is included by mistake.

No through road
Photo © Stephen Aaron Rees
Used under licence from Shutterstock.com

In many cases these routes are fine and could save you a lot of unnecessary distance, but inappropriate short cuts could cause you a lot of trouble, particularly if you are in a larger vehicle. So here are a few tips to avoid inappropriate short cuts:

- Always take notice of road signs. They are there for a reason, and the people who put them there have better local knowledge than your Sat Nav data provider. Look out particularly for these signs and don't go past them unless you're nearing your destination:

No motor vehicles
Photo © Paul Fleet
Used under licence from Shutterstock.com

- o 'No through road'
- o 'Unsuitable for motor vehicles' (or 'Unsuitable for wide/ heavy/long/high vehicles' if you're in one.)
- o 'Sat Nav error' or 'Do not follow Sat Nav' signs. These signs have been put up in a few 'hotspots', such as supposed short cuts across rivers where there is no bridge or ferry, and narrow lanes where lorries keep getting stuck.

- Never leave tarmac - unless of course you're heading for an off-road destination and you're nearly there.

- If you do get stuck up a dead end on an inappropriate short cut, try to:

  - o Turn round where you can.

  - o Stop and look at the map.

  - o Find an intermediate destination – a place you need to go through – and reset your route to this place.

  - o When you reach your intermediate destination, reset your route to your final destination.

The golden rule is: **Don't do anything you wouldn't do if you didn't have a Sat Nav.** So if you reach a ford and the stream is swollen, don't cross it even if the Sat Nav directs you that way.

Driving with your Sat Nav

- It can be very easy to be distracted from what's going on around you by all the information available on a Sat Nav display. Some models allow the map display to be turned off so there are only audible instructions which may be wise if you are prone to staring at the screen.

- It can be tempting to use the Sat Nav whilst on the move, particularly if you want it to calculate a new route for you but this can be highly distracting and dangerous. It's much better to pull over in a safe place before attempting to programme it.

- Remember just because your Sat Nav tells you to do something it is does not mean it is necessarily safe to do so in the current conditions. Being told to leave the motorway at the next junction does not mean it is wise to pull into the left lane immediately without checking that there is nothing in the way.

- Even when the mapping in a Sat Nav is regularly updated there are always changes that will have happened in the real world since the device was updated - new roads will open, others will be closed off, speed limits will change etc.

> At all times pay attention to the road signs, road layout and conditions around you.

Entering your Destination into your Sat Nav

It's easy to make simple spelling mistakes or enter postcodes incorrectly which will end up with you being directed to the wrong place, so be as careful as you can. Duplicated street names or place names are a particular problem – just which 'Church Road' do you want in which 'Newport'? If you know the full postcode of your destination it is wisest to use that as postcodes aren't duplicated around the country.

Then before you set off, check that the 'distance to destination' is about what you expect. If you're only expecting to travel across town to the cinema you don't want to find you're heading up the motorway to a cinema 200 miles away by mistake! And be particularly careful if you have maps of the whole of Europe – one lorry driver heading from Turkey to Gibraltar once ended up at Gibraltar Point near Skegness in Lincolnshire.

> The golden rule is: Always Sense Check your Sat Nav

Reducing the risk of theft

Sat Nav systems are a target for opportunist thieves and the theft of devices is reportedly on the increase. Portable systems that clip into a dashboard cradle are particularly susceptible to theft. There are basic steps to reduce the risk of being a victim of these crimes:

- Do not leave the cradle attached to the windscreen or dashboard when you leave the vehicle. Thieves may break in to see if the device has been left in the boot or glove box (*see photo opposite*).

- Remove any tell-tale suction marks on the windscreen that may indicate a device has been used in the vehicle. Thieves frequently break in to see if any equipment has been hidden from sight.

- Ideally do not hide the equipment in the glove box or boot. Thieves will usually look for it there. Carry it with you if you can.

Photo © Shevelev Vladimir
Used under licence from Shutterstock.com

- Consider a device with a lock system requiring a pin number to operate. If stolen these cannot be operated, thus deterring potential thieves.

- Mark your equipment with your postcode and vehicle registration using a security marker. This will make it easier to identify lost or stolen devices.

- Keep a record of the make, model and serial number of your equipment. Owners of Sat Navs are also encouraged to register details of their system on-line at www.immobilise.com. This is the UK's national property register. Registration is free and the register is used by all UK police forces to trace owners of lost and stolen property.

Sat Nav for large vehicles

There are frequent press reports of lorries or large vehicles getting wedged under a bridge or stranded in a field as a result of blindly following the Sat Nav instructions. It has been estimated (Network Rail, 2008) that over 2000 bridges a year are damaged in this way. These are examples of drivers of large commercial vehicles using satellite navigation systems designed for cars. If you drive a wide, heavy or long vehicle such as a van, lorry or bus then you need to be particularly careful when choosing and using a Sat Nav.

Dedicated 'truck Sat Nav' systems are available and these have been designed especially for large commercial vehicles – lorries, HGVs, coaches, buses, caravans and mobile homes. Sat Nav technology on these includes height, width and weight limits to generate tailor made HGV friendly routes avoiding low bridges and weight restricted roads based on the size and weight load of specific vehicles. Places of interest (POIs) are also available specifically for commercial users - including truck stops, truck restaurants and petrol stations suitable for trucks.

Using this atlas with your Sat Nav

- The detailed route planning maps in this atlas are particularly useful for getting an overview of your longer journeys. It's a good idea to know before starting your journey whether you've got 100 miles of motorway driving followed by 20 miles of country roads or 60 miles driving through heavily built up and congested areas. The screen on even the higher quality Sat Nav devices is quite small so it can be very difficult to visualise your entire route before setting off using the Sat Nav alone.

- The maps in this atlas also allow you to see what's around you, not only on your journey but also when you reach your destination. If you've gone away for a weekend the maps allow you to get an idea of the lie of the land, to pick out which tourist attractions you'd like to visit and which places it would be sensible to visit on the same day.

- If you've got a long journey ahead and you'd like to stop somewhere on the way for a rest this atlas makes it easy to spot a handy town or attraction you could visit or even which motorway service area is most appropriate.

- Entering a postcode into your Sat Nav is the easiest way to locate something and so we've provided you with full postcodes for a large number of places of interest scattered throughout the country.

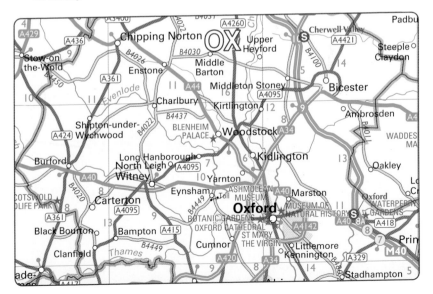

One of the easiest ways to locate something using a Sat Nav is to input the postcode of the location you are looking for. The following pages list popular destinations along with full postcodes (always shown in **bold** type) and an atlas reference (not all locations appear on the map).

In all instances when getting close to your destination follow local road signs to lead you to the precise location you require.

Tourist attractions

1000 tourist attractions spread right across Great Britian are listed below. If you know the name of the attraction you are looking for then search for it in the alphabetical listing below and put the full postcode into your Sat Nav. Alternatively use the map pages in this atlas to locate tourist attractions within your area of interest before looking up their postcodes in this list. To locate an attraction within this atlas use the reference given in brackets e.g. 1853 Gallery can be found on page 24 in grid square A3.

To make it easier to find a particular type of attraction in the list, e.g. a theme park, each attraction is colour-coded.
Country park – brown
Garden – green
Historic attraction – purple
Museum or art gallery – orange
Sport or event venue – cyan
Theme park – red
All others – black

1853 Gallery
WYorks (24 A3) **BD18 3LA**

Abbotsbury Swannery & Sub Tropical Gardens
Dorset **DT3 4JG**

Aberdeen Art Gallery
Aberdeen (41 G5) **AB10 1FQ**

Aberdeen Exhibition & Conference Centre
Aberdeen (41 G5) **AB23 8BL**

Aberglasney Gardens
Carmar (11 E3) **SA32 8QH**

Aberystwyth Arts Centre
Cere (16 C6) **SY23 3DE**

Aden Country Park
Aber (41 G3) **AB42 5FQ**

Adventure Island
S'end (15 E5) **SS1 1EE**

Adventure Wonderland
Dorset **BH23 6BA**

Afan Argoed Country Park
NPT (11 F5) **SA13 3HG**

Afonwen Craft & Antique Centre
Flints (22 B6) **CH7 5UB**

Africa Alive! *Suff* **NR33 7TF**

Albert Park
Middl (29 E5) **TS1 3LB**

Aldenham Country Park
Herts **WD6 3AT**

Alexandra Palace
GtLon **N22 7AY**

Allensford Country Park
Dur **DH8 9BA**

Almondell & Calderwood Country Park
WLoth (32 B2) **EH52 5PE**

Alnwick Garden, The
N'umb (33 H5) **NE66 1YU**

Althorp House
N'hants **NN7 4HQ**

Alton Towers Leisure Park
Staffs (18 C2) **ST10 4DB**

Alton Water Reservoir
Suff (15 G3) **IP9 2RY**

Amerton Farm
Staffs (18 C3) **ST18 0LA**

Anderton Boat Lift
ChesW&C **CW9 6FW**

Anglers Country Park
WYorks **WF4 2EB**

Anglesey Abbey
Cambs **CB25 9EJ**

Anglesey Sea Zoo
IoA (16 B2) **LL61 6TQ**

Animal World & Butterfly House *GtMan* **BL1 5UG**

Anne Hathaway's Cottage
Warks (13 E2) **CV37 9HH**

Aonach Mòr Mountain Gondola & Nevis Range Ski Centre
High (35 G1) **PH33 6SW**

Argyll & Sutherland Highlanders Museum
Stir **FK8 1EH**

Arnolfini Gallery
Bristol (12 B6) **BS1 4QA**

Aros Experience
High (38 B3) **IV51 9EU**

Arundel Castle
WSuss **BN18 9AB**

Arundel Cathedral (R.C.)
WSuss **BN18 9AY**

Ashmolean Museum
Oxon (13 G4) **OX1 2PH**

Ashridge Estate
Herts (14 A4) **HP4 1LX**

Ashton Court Estate
NSom (12 B6) **BS41 9JN**

Attingham Park *Shrop* **SY4 4TP**

Aviation Viewing Park
GtMan (23 E5) **M90 1QX**

Avon Heath Country Park
Dorset (7 E4) **BH24 2DA**

Avon Valley Railway
SGlos **BS30 6HD**

Babbacombe Model Village
Torbay (5 F5) **TQ1 3LA**

Baddesley Clinton
Warks **B93 0DQ**

Baggeridge Country Park
Staffs **DY3 4HB**

Balmedie Country Park
Aber (41 G5) **AB23 8XG**

Bamburgh Castle
N'umb **NE69 7DF**

Banbury Museum
Oxon (13 F3) **OX16 2PQ**

Banham Zoo
Norf (21 E5) **NR16 2HE**

Barbican Arts & Conference Centre *GtLon* **EC2Y 8DS**

Barnwell Country Park
N'hants (19 H5) **PE8 5PB**

Barry Island Pleasure Park
VGlam (11 H6) **CF62 5TR**

Barter Books, Alnwick
N'umb (33 H5) **NE66 2NP**

Bath Abbey
B&NESom (12 C6) **BA1 1LT**
Battersea Cats & Dogs Home
GtLon **SW8 4AA**
Battersea Park Children's Zoo
GtLon **SW11 4NJ**
Battle Abbey *ESuss* **TN33 0AD**
Baxters Highland Village
Moray (40 D2) **IV32 7LD**
Beacon Fell Country Park
Lancs (22 D2) **PR3 2NL**
Beacon Hill Country Park
Leics (19 F4) **LE12 8SR**
Beacon Park, Up Holland
Lancs **WN8 7RU**
Beale Park *WBerks* **RG8 9NH**
Beamish, North of England
Open Air Museum
Dur (28 D3) **DH9 0RG**
Beatles Story *Mersey* **L3 4AD**
Beaulieu:
National Motor Museum,
Abbey & Palace House
Hants (7 F4) **SO42 7ZN**
Beaumaris Castle
IoA (16 C2) **LL58 8AP**
Beecraigs Country Park
WLoth (32 B2) **EH49 6PL**
Bekonscot Model Village
Bucks (14 A5) **HP9 2PL**
Belton House *Lincs* **NG32 2LS**
Bestwood Country Park
Notts (19 F2) **NG6 8UF**
Bewl Water
ESuss (8 D4) **TN3 8JH**
Bicton Park Gardens
Devon (5 F4) **EX9 7BJ**
Big Pit National Coal Museum
Torfaen (11 H4) **NP4 9XP**
Big Sheep, The
Devon **EX39 5AP**
Big Sky Adventure Play
Peter **PE2 7BU**
Birdworld, Farnham
Hants **GU10 4LD**
Birmingham Botanical Gardens
WMid **B15 3TR**
Birmingham City Museum &
Art Gallery
WMid (18 C5) **B3 3DH**
Black Country Living Museum
WMid (18 C5) **DY1 4SQ**
Black Park Country Park
Bucks (14 A5) **SL3 6DR**
Black Sheep Brewery Visitor
Centre *NYorks* **HG4 4EN**
Black Swan Guild, Frome
Som **BA11 1BB**
Blackgang Chine
IoW (7 F6) **PO38 2HN**

Blackpool Piers
B'pool (22 C3) **FY4 1BB**
Blackpool Pleasure Beach
B'pool (22 C3) **FY4 1PL**
Blackpool Tower
B'pool (22 C3) **FY1 4BJ**
Blackpool Zoo
B'pool (22 C3) **FY3 8PP**
Blair Castle
P&K (36 B1) **PH18 5TL**
Blair Drummond Safari &
Adventure Park
Stir (32 A1) **FK9 4UR**
Blake House Craft Centre
Essex **CM77 6RA**
Blakemere Shopping Experience
ChesW&C (22 D6) **CW8 2EB**
Blenheim Palace
Oxon (13 F4) **OX20 1PX**
Blue Planet Aquarium,
Ellesmere Port
ChesW&C (22 C6) **CH65 9LF**
Blue Reef Aquarium
ESuss **TN34 3DW**
Blue Reef Aquarium, Newquay
Corn (3 G3) **TR7 1DU**
Blue Reef Aquarium, Southsea
Ports **PO5 3PB**
Blue Reef Aquarium, Tynemouth
T&W (29 E2) **NE30 4JF**
Bluebell Railway
WSuss (8 C4) **TN22 3QL**
Bodiam Castle *ESuss* **TN32 5UA**
Bodleian Library *Oxon* **OX1 3BG**
Bodnant Garden
Conwy (16 D2) **LL28 5RE**
Bolam Lake Country Park
N'umb **NE20 0HE**
Bolton Abbey Estate
NYorks (23 F2) **BD23 6EX**
Bolton Museum & Art Gallery
GtMan **BL1 1SE**
Bolton Priory *NYorks* **BD23 6EX**
Boscastle Pottery
Corn (4 B4) **PL35 0HE**
Bosworth Battlefield Country Park
Leics (19 E4) **CV13 0AD**
Botanic Garden, Oxford
Oxon (13 G4) **OX1 4AZ**
Botany Bay
Lancs (22 D4) **PR6 9AF**
Bournemouth
International Centre
Bourne (6 D5) **BH2 5BH**
Bowood House & Gardens
Wilts **SN11 0LZ**
Bradford Cathedral Church of
St. Peter *WYorks* **BD1 4EH**
Bradgate Park
Leics (19 F4) **LE6 0HE**

Brampton Valley Way
Country Park
N'hants (13 H1) **NN6 9DG**
Brandon Park *Suff* **IP27 0SU**
Brandon to Bishop Auckland Walk
Dur **DH7 7RJ**
Branston Water Park
Staffs **DE14 3EZ**
Brecon Beacons Visitor Centre
Powys (11 G3) **LD3 8ER**
Brecon Mountain Railway
MTyd (11 G4) **CF48 2UP**
Bressingham Steam Museum &
Gardens *Norf* **IP22 2AA**
Brickfields Horse Country
IoW **PO33 3TH**
Bridgewater Hall, Manchester
GtMan **M2 3WS**
Bridgnorth Cliff Railway
Shrop (18 B5) **WV16 4AH**
Brighton Centre, The
B&H (8 C5) **BN1 2GR**
Brighton Museum &
Art Gallery *B&H* **BN1 1EE**
Brighton Pier
B&H (8 C5) **BN2 1TW**
Bristol Cathedral
Bristol **BS1 5TJ**
Bristol City Museum &
Art Gallery
Bristol (12 B6) **BS8 1RL**
Bristol Zoo
Bristol (12 B6) **BS8 3HA**
Britain At War Experience
GtLon **SE1 2TF**
British Empire &
Commonwealth Museum
Bristol **BS1 6QH**
British Library (St. Pancras)
GtLon **NW1 2DB**
British Museum
GtLon (14 C5) **WC1B 3DG**
Brixworth Country Park
N'hants (13 H1) **NN6 9DG**
Brontë Weaving Shed
WYorks **BD22 8EP**
Brooklands Museum
Surr **KT13 0QN**
Brookside Miniature Railway
ChesE **SK12 1BZ**
Brougham Hall
Cumb **CA10 2DE**
Brownsea Island
Dorset **BH13 7EE**
Brymor Ice Cream
NYorks (28 D6) **HG4 4PG**
Bryn Bach Country Park
BGwent (11 H4) **NP22 3AY**
Buckfast Abbey
Devon (5 E5) **TQ11 0EE**

Buckingham Palace
GtLon **SW1A 1AA**
Burbage Common
Leics **LE10 3DD**
Bure Valley Railway
Norf **NR11 6BW**
Burns National Heritage Park
SAyr (31 G6) **KA7 4PQ**
Burrell Collection
Glas (31 H3) **G43 1AT**
Business Design Centre,
Islington *GtLon* **N1 0QH**

Cadbury World
WMid (18 C5) **B30 1JR**
Caernarfon Castle
Gwyn (16 B2) **LL55 2AY**
Caerphilly Castle
Caerp (11 H5) **CF83 1JD**
Cairngorm Mountain
High (40 B5) **PH22 1RB**
Caithness Crystal Visitor Centre
Norf **PE30 4NE**
Calderglen Country Park
SLan (31 H4) **G75 0QZ**
California Country Park
W'ham (13 H6) **RG40 4HT**
Cambridge American Military
Cemetery & Memorial
Cambs **CB23 7PH**
Cambridge University Botanic
Garden *Cambs* **CB2 1JF**
Camel Trail
Corn (3 H3) **PL27 7AL**
Camelot Theme Park
Lancs **PR7 5LP**
Camperdown Country Park
Dundee (37 E3) **DD2 4TF**
Cannon Hall Country Park
SYorks (24 A4) **S75 4AT**
Cannon Hall Farm
SYorks (24 A4) **S75 4AT**
Cannon Hill Park
WMid (18 C5) **B13 8RD**
Canterbury Cathedral
Kent (9 G3) **CT1 2EH**
Cardiff Bay Visitor Centre
Cardiff (11 H6) **CF10 4PA**
Cardiff Castle & Museum
Cardiff (11 H6) **CF10 3RB**
Cardiff Millennium Stadium
Cardiff (11 H6) **CF10 1GE**
Carisbrooke Castle & Museum
IoW **PO30 1XY**
Carlisle Cathedral
Cumb **CA3 8TZ**
Carlisle Park, Morpeth
N'umb (28 D1) **NE61 1YD**
Carsington Water
Derbys (18 D2) **DE6 1ST**

Cascades Adventure Pool
Devon **EX33 1NZ**
Castell Coch
Cardiff (11 H5) **CF15 7JQ**
Castle Drogo *Devon* **EX6 6PB**
Castle Eden Dene National
Nature Reserve *Dur* **SR8 1NJ**
Castle Howard
NYorks (24 D1) **YO60 7DA**
Castle Semple Water Country
Park *Renf* (31 G4) **PA12 4HJ**
Causey Arch Picnic Area
Dur **NE16 5EG**
CC2000
Pembs (10 B4) **SA67 8DD**
Centre for Alternative
Technology, Machynlleth
Powys (16 D5) **SY20 9AZ**
Centre for Life,
Newcastle upon Tyne
T&W **NE1 4EP**
Ceramica *Stoke* **ST6 3DS**
Chartwell
Kent (8 C3) **TN16 1PS**
Chatelherault Country Park
SLan (32 A3) **ML3 7UE**
Chatham Historic Dockyard
Med **ME4 4TZ**
Chatsworth Farmyard &
Adventure Playground
Derbys **DE45 1PP**
Chatsworth House
Derbys (24 A6) **DE45 1PP**
Cheddar Gorge & Caves
Som (6 A2) **BS27 3QF**
Chepstow Castle
Mon (12 B5) **NP16 5EY**
Cheshire Farm Ice Cream,
Tattenhall
ChesW&C (17 G3) **CH3 9NE**
Chessington World of Adventures
GtLon (14 B6) **KT9 2NE**
Chester Cathedral
ChesW&C (22 C6) **CH1 2HU**
Chester Zoo
ChesW&C (22 C6) **CH2 1LH**
Chevin Forest Park
WYorks (24 A2) **LS21 3JL**
Chichester Cathedral
WSuss **PO19 1PX**
Chirk Castle
Wrex (17 F4) **LL14 5AF**
Christ Church, Oxford
Oxon **OX1 1DP**
Church of St. Mary-in-Castro,
Dover *Kent* (9 H3) **CT16 1HU**
Churchill Museum & Cabinet
War Rooms *GtLon* **SW1A 2AQ**
Clacton Pier
Essex (15 G4) **CO15 1QX**

Clambers Play Centre, Hastings
ESuss (9 E5) **TN34 1LD**
Clare Castle Country Park
Suff (15 E2) **CO10 8NJ**
Claremont Landscape Garden
Surr **KT10 9JG**
Cleethorpes Discovery Centre
NELincs (25 G4) **DN35 0AG**
Clent Hills Country Park
Worcs (18 C5) **DY9 9JR**
Cliff Railway, Aberystwyth
Cere (16 C6) **SY23 2DN**
Clifford's Tower *York* **YO1 9SA**
Cliveden
Bucks (14 A5) **SL6 0JA**
Clovelly Village
Devon (4 C2) **EX39 5TA**
Clumber Country Park
Notts (24 C6) **S80 3AZ**
Cockington Country Park
Torbay (5 E5) **TQ2 6XA**
Coed y Brenin Forest Park
Gwyn (16 D4) **LL40 2HY**
Colchester Castle Museum
Essex **CO1 1TJ**
Colchester Zoo
Essex (15 F3) **CO3 0SL**
Colony Gift Corporation
Cumb (22 B1) **LA12 0LD**
Colston Hall *Bristol* **BS1 5AR**
Combe Martin Wildlife &
Dinosaur Park
Devon (4 D1) **EX34 0NG**
Conkers, Swadlincote
Leics **DE12 6GA**
Conwy Castle
Conwy (16 D2) **LL32 8LD**
Coombe Country Park
Warks (13 F1) **CV3 2AB**
Corfe Castle
Dorset (6 D5) **BH20 5EZ**
Corn Exchange, Cambridge
Cambs (14 C2) **CB2 3QB**
Cornish Gold & Treasure Park
Corn (3 F4) **TR16 4HN**
Corris Craft Centre
Gwyn (16 D5) **SY20 9RF**
Cosmeston Lakes Country Park
VGlam (11 H6) **CF64 5UY**
Cotswold Water Park
Glos (13 E5) **GL7 6DF**
Cotswold Wildlife Park
Oxon (13 E4) **OX18 4JP**
Courtauld Institute of
Art Gallery *GtLon* **WC2R 0RN**
Coventry Cathedral
WMid (13 F1) **CV1 5AB**
Coventry Transport Museum
WMid (13 F1) **CV1 1JD**
Cragside *N'umb* **NE65 7PX**

ix

Crealy Adventure Park Devon
Devon (5 F4) **EX5 1DR**
Crich Tramway Village
Derbys **DE4 5DP**
Crickley Hill Country Park
Glos (12 D4) **GL4 8JY**
Crieff Visitor Centre & Caithness
Glass *P&K* **PH7 4HQ**
Crombie Country Park
Angus **DD5 3QL**
Croxteth Country Park
Mersey **L12 0HB**
Croxteth Hall
Mersey **L12 0HB**
Crystal Palace Park
GtLon **SE20 8DT**
Cudmore Grove Country Park
Essex **CO5 8UE**
Culzean Castle & Country Park
SAyr (31 F6) **KA19 8LE**

Dalby Forest Drive
NYorks (29 G6) **YO18 7LT**
Dare Valley Country Park
RCT (11 G4) **CF44 7RG**
Dartington Cider Press Centre
Devon (5 E5) **TQ9 6TQ**
Dartington Crystal Ltd.
Devon (4 C3) **EX38 7AN**
Daventry Country Park
N'hants (13 G1) **NN11 2JB**
David Marshall Lodge
Stir (31 H1) **FK8 3SX**
Dean Castle & Country Park
EAyr (31 G5) **KA3 1XB**
Dean Gallery *Edin* **EH4 3DS**
Deep Sea World,
North Queensferry
Fife (32 C1) **KY11 1JR**
Deep, The *Hull* **HU1 4DP**
Deerness Valley Walk
Dur **DH7 7RJ**
Denbies Wine Estate
Surr (8 B3) **RH5 6AA**
Denby Pottery
Derbys (19 E2) **DE5 8NX**
Derby City Museum &
Art Gallery *Derby* **DE1 1BS**
Derwent Walk Country Park
Dur (28 D3) **NE16 3BN**
Devon Guild of Craftsmen
Devon **TQ13 9AF**
Dick Institute
EAyr **KA1 3BU**
Dinosaur Adventure Park
Norf **NR9 5JW**
Dinosaur Museum, Dorchester
Dorset **DT1 1EW**
Dinton Pastures Country Park
W'ham (13 H6) **RG10 0TH**

Discovery Museum,
Newcastle upon Tyne
T&W (28 D2) **NE1 4JA**
Dock Museum, Barrow-in-Furness
Cumb **LA14 2PW**
Doncaster Racecourse
Exhibition Centre
SYorks (24 C4) **DN2 6BB**
Donkey Sanctuary,
Salcombe Regis
Devon (5 G4) **EX10 0NU**
Dorchester Abbey
Oxon **OX10 7HH**
Dover Castle
Kent (9 H3) **CT16 1HU**
Drayton Manor Park
Staffs (18 D4) **B78 3TW**
Drumpellier Country Park
NLan (32 A2) **ML5 1RX**
Druridge Bay Country Park
N'umb **NE61 5BX**
Drusillas Park
ESuss (8 D5) **BN26 5QS**
Dudley Zoo & Castle
WMid (18 C5) **DY1 4QB**
Dundee Contemporary Arts
Dundee (37 E3) **DD1 4DY**
Dunham Massey Hall,
Park & Gardens
GtMan **WA14 4SJ**
Dunstable Downs
CenBeds (14 A3) **LU6 2GY**
Dunster Castle & Gardens
Som **TA24 6SL**
Durham Cathedral
Dur (28 D3) **DH1 3EH**
Durham Dales Centre
Dur **DL13 2FJ**
Durlston Country Park
Dorset (6 D6) **BH19 2JL**
Duthie Park & David Welch
Winter Gardens
Aberdeen (41 G5) **AB11 7TH**
Dylan Thomas Centre
Swan (11 E5) **SA1 1RR**
Dyrham Park *SGlos* **SN14 8ER**

Earls Court Exhibition Centre
GtLon (14 B6) **SW5 9TA**
East Carlton Countryside Park
N'hants (19 G5) **LE16 8YF**
East Lancashire Railway
Lancs **BL9 0EY**
East Point Pavilion, Lowestoft
Suff (21 H5) **NR33 0AP**
Eastbourne Pier
ESuss (8 D6) **BN21 3EL**
Eden Camp *NYorks* **YO17 6RT**
Eden Project
Corn (3 H4) **PL24 2SG**

Edinburgh Castle
Edin (32 C2) **EH1 2NG**
Edinburgh Zoo
Edin (32 C2) **EH12 6TS**
Eilean Donan Castle
High (38 D4) **IV40 8DX**
Elan Valley Visitor Centre
Powys (11 G1) **LD6 5HP**
Electric Mountain, Llanberis
Gwyn (16 C2) **LL55 4UR**
Eling Tide Mill
Hants **SO40 9HF**
Elsecar Heritage Centre
SYorks **S74 8HJ**
Elvaston Castle Country Park
Derbys (19 E3) **DE72 3EP**
Emberton Country Park
MK **MK46 5FJ**
Embsay Steam Railway
NYorks **BD23 6AF**
Erddig *Wrex (17 G3)* **LL13 0YT**
Etherow Country Park
GtMan (23 F5) **SK6 5JQ**
Eureka! Museum for Children
WYorks (23 F3) **HX1 2NE**
Evesham Country Park
Shopping & Garden Centre
Worcs (12 D2) **WR11 4TP**
Exbury Gardens
Hants **SO45 1AZ**
Exeter Cathedral
Devon (5 F4) **EX1 1HS**
Explore-At-Bristol
Bristol **BS1 5DB**

Fairfield Halls, Croydon
GtLon (14 C6) **CR9 1DG**
Fairlands Valley Park
Herts (14 B3) **SG2 0BL**
Falkirk Wheel
Falk (32 A1) **FK1 4RS**
Famous Grouse Experience,
Glenturret Distillery
P&K (36 B3) **PH7 4HA**
Fantasy Island
Lincs (25 H6) **PE25 1RH**
Ferens Art Gallery
Hull **HU1 3RA**
Ferrers Centre for Arts & Crafts
Leics **LE65 1RU**
Festival Park
BGwent (11 H4) **NP23 8FP**
Ffestiniog Railway
Gwyn (16 C3) **LL49 9NF**
Fishers Farm Park
WSuss **RH14 0EG**
Fitzwilliam Museum
Cambs (14 C2) **CB2 1RB**
Flambards Experience, The
Corn (3 F5) **TR13 0QA**

Flamingo Land Theme Park
NYorks (29 G6) **YO17 6UX**

Flamingo Park, Hastings
ESuss (9 E5) **TN34 3AR**

Flatts Lane Woodland
Country Park *R&C* **TS6 0NN**

Fleet Air Arm Museum
Som **BA22 8HT**

Folly Farm, Begelly
Pembs (10 C4) **SA68 0XA**

Foremark Reservoir
Derbys (19 E3) **DE65 6EG**

Forfar Loch Country Park
Angus (37 E2) **DD8 1BT**

Fort Fun, Eastbourne
ESuss (8 D5) **BN22 7LQ**

Foxton Locks
Leics (19 F5) **LE16 7RA**

French Brothers Cruises
W&M (14 A6) **SL4 5JH**

Friars, The, Aylesford
Kent (9 E3) **ME20 7BX**

Fruitmarket Gallery
Edin **EH1 1DF**

Fun Farm, Spalding
Lincs **PE12 6JU**

Gallery of Modern Art
Glas (31 H3) **G1 3AH**

Garwnant Visitor Centre
MTyd (11 G4) **CF48 2HU**

Gelli Aur Country Park
Carmar (11 E3) **SA32 8LR**

Gibraltar Point National
Nature Reserve
Lincs (20 C2) **PE24 4SU**

Gibside *T&W* **NE16 6BG**

Glamis Castle *Angus* **DD8 1QJ**

Glasgow Botanic Garden
Glas **G12 0UE**

Glasgow Royal Concert Hall
Glas **G2 3NY**

Glasgow Science Centre
Glas **G51 1EA**

Glass Studio, Eastbourne Pier
ESuss (8 D6) **BN21 3EL**

Glastonbury Abbey
Som **BA6 9EL**

Glencoe Visitor Centre
High **PH49 4LA**

Gleniffer Braes Country Park
Renf (31 G3) **PA2 8TE**

Glenmore Forest Park
Visitor Centre *High* **PH22 1QY**

Glentress Forest
ScBord (32 C3) **EH45 8NB**

Gloucester Cathedral
Glos (12 C4) **GL1 2LR**

Gloucester Historic Docks
Glos (12 C4) **GL1 2ER**

Gloucestershire & Warwickshire
Railway *Glos* **GL54 5DT**

Go Bananas, Colchester
Essex (15 F3) **CO1 1BX**

Godstone Farm
Surr (8 C3) **RH9 8LX**

Golden Acre Park
WYorks (24 A2) **LS16 8BQ**

Goleulong 2000 Lightship
Cardiff (11 H6) **CF10 4PA**

Grafham Water
Cambs (14 B1) **PE28 0BH**

Grand Pier, Teignmouth
Devon (5 F5) **TQ14 8BB**

Great Aberystwyth
Camera Obscura
Cere (16 C6) **SY23 2DN**

Great Hall, Winchester
Hants **SO23 8UJ**

Great Orme Tramway
Conwy (16 D1) **LL30 2HG**

Great St. Mary's Church,
Cambridge *Cambs* **CB2 3PQ**

Greenmeadow Community Farm
Torfaen (11 H5) **NP44 5AJ**

Grizedale Forest Park
Cumb (27 H6) **LA22 0QJ**

Groombridge Place Gardens
Kent **TN3 9QG**

Guildford House Gallery
Surr **GU1 3AJ**

Gullane Bents
ELoth (32 D1) **EH31 2AZ**

Haddo Country Park
Aber (41 F4) **AB41 7EQ**

Hadleigh Castle Country Park
Essex (15 E5) **SS7 2PP**

Haigh Hall Country Park
GtMan (22 D4) **WN2 1PE**

Hainault Forest Country Park
Essex (14 C5) **IG7 4QN**

Ham Hill Country Park
Som (6 A4) **TA14 6RW**

Hammersmith Apollo
GtLon **W6 9QH**

Hampden Park Stadium
Glas **G42 9BA**

Hampton Court Palace &
Garden *GtLon* **KT8 9AU**

Hamsterley Forest
Dur (28 C4) **DL13 3NL**

Harbour Park Amusements,
Littlehampton
WSuss (8 A5) **BN17 5LL**

Hardwick Hall
Derbys **S44 5QJ**

Hardwick Hall Country Park,
Sedgefield
Dur (29 E4) **TS21 2EH**

Harewood House
WYorks (24 B2) **LS17 9LG**

Harlech Castle
Gwyn (16 C4) **LL46 2YH**

Harris Museum & Art Gallery,
Preston *Lancs* **PR1 2PP**

Harrogate International Centre
NYorks (24 A2) **HG1 5LA**

Harrold-Odell Country Park
Bed (14 A2) **MK43 7DS**

Harrow Museum
GtLon **HA2 6PX**

Hartlepool's Maritime Experience
Hart **TS24 0XZ**

Hartsholme Country Park
Lincs (25 E6) **LN6 0EY**

Hastings Fishermen's Museum
ESuss **TN34 3DW**

Hatton Country World
Warks (13 E1) **CV35 8XA**

Hayward Gallery
GtLon **SE1 8XZ**

Healey's Cornish Cyder Farm
Corn (3 G4) **TR4 9LW**

Heart of the Country Centre
Staffs (18 D4) **WS14 9QR**

Heatherton Activity Park
Pembs (10 B4) **SA70 8RJ**

Heaton Park
GtMan (23 E4) **M25 2SW**

Hereford Cathedral
Here (12 B3) **HR1 2NG**

Heritage Motor Centre, Gaydon
Warks **CV35 0BJ**

Hever Castle & Gardens
Kent (8 C3) **TN8 7NG**

Hexham Abbey
N'umb **NE46 3NB**

Hidcote Manor Garden
Glos **GL55 6LR**

High Lodge Forest Centre
Suff **IP27 0AF**

High Moorland Visitor Centre,
Princetown *Devon* **PL20 6QF**

High Woods Country Park
Essex **CO4 5JR**

Himley Hall & Park
WMid (18 B5) **DY3 4DF**

H.M.S. Belfast *GtLon* **SE1 2JH**

H.M.S. Victory
Ports (7 G4) **PO1 3PX**

H.M.S. Warrior
Ports (7 G4) **PO1 3QX**

Hoar Park Craft Centre
Warks **CV10 0QU**

Holy Trinity Church,
Skipton *NYorks* **BD23 1NJ**

Holy Trinity Church,
Stratford-upon-Avon
Warks (13 E2) **CV37 6BG**

Holywell Bay Fun Park
Corn **TR8 5PW**
Hop Farm, The
Kent (8 D3) **TN12 6PY**
Hop Pocket, The *Here* **WR6 5BT**
Horniman Museum
GtLon **SE23 3PQ**
Hornsea Freeport
ERid (25 F2) **HU18 1UT**
Horton Park Farm
Surr **KT19 8PT**
House of Marbles &
Teign Valley Glass
Devon (5 E5) **TQ13 9DS**
Howletts Wild Animal Park
Kent (9 G3) **CT4 5EL**
Humber Bridge Country Park
ERid **HU13 0LN**
Hylands Park
Essex (14 D4) **CM2 8WQ**

Ightham Mote
Kent **TN15 0NT**
Imperial War Museum, Duxford
Cambs (14 C2) **CB22 4QR**
Imperial War Museum, London
GtLon **SE1 6HZ**
Imperial War Museum North
GtMan **M17 1TZ**
Intech, Winchester
Hants **SO21 1HX**
International Centre, The, Telford
Tel&W (18 B4) **TF3 4JH**
Irchester Country Park
N'hants (14 A1) **NN29 7DL**
Ironbridge Gorge
Tel&W (18 A4) **TF8 7DQ**
Isle of Bute Discovery Centre
A&B **PA20 0AH**
Isle of Wight Pearl
IoW (7 F5) **PO30 4DD**
Isle of Wight Zoo
IoW **PO36 8QB**
Itchen Valley Country Park
Hants (7 F4) **SO30 3HQ**

James Hamilton Heritage Park
SLan **G74 5LB**
James Pringle Weavers of
Inverness *High* **IV2 4RB**
Jephson Gardens
Warks (13 F1) **CV32 4ER**
Jinney Ring Craft Centre, The
Worcs (12 D1) **B60 4BU**
Jodrell Bank Observatory &
Arboretum *ChesE* **SK11 9DL**
John Muir Country Park
ELoth (33 E2) **EH42 1UW**

Johnstons Cashmere
Visitor Centre
Moray (40 C2) **IV30 4AF**
Jorvik *York* (24 C2) **YO1 9WT**
Jorvik Glass
NYorks (24 D1) **YO60 7DA**

Kathellan *Fife* (32 C1) **KY4 0JR**
Kelvingrove Art Gallery & Museum
Glas (31 H3) **G3 8AG**
Kenilworth Castle
Warks **CV8 1NE**
Kensington Palace
GtLon **W8 4PX**
Kenwood House
GtLon **NW3 7JR**
Kielder Forest
N'umb (28 A1) **NE48 1ER**
Kielder Water
N'umb (28 B1) **NE48 1BX**
Killerton *Devon* **EX5 3LE**
King's College Chapel, Cambridge
Cambs (14 C2) **CB2 1ST**
Kingsbury Water Park
Warks (18 D5) **B76 0DY**
Kingston Lacy
Dorset (6 D4) **BH21 4EA**
Kit Hill Country Park
Corn **PL17 8AX**
Knebworth House
Herts **SG3 6PY**
Knettishall Heath Country Park
Suff **IP22 2TQ**
Knowsley Safari Park
Mersey (22 C5) **L34 4AN**

Lace Market Centre
Nott **NG1 1HF**
Lady Lever Art Gallery
Mersey **CH62 5EQ**
Laing Art Gallery,
Newcastle upon Tyne
T&W (28 D2) **NE1 8AG**
Lake District Visitor Centre
at Brockhole
Cumb (27 H5) **LA23 1LJ**
Lakes Aquarium
Cumb (27 H6) **LA12 8AS**
Lakes Glass Centre, Ulverston
Cumb **LA12 7LY**
Lakeside & Haverthwaite
Railway *Cumb* **LA12 8AL**
Lancaster Leisure Park
Lancs (22 C1) **LA1 3LA**
Lancaster Priory
Lancs **LA1 1YZ**
Land's End
Corn (3 E5) **TR19 7AA**
Langdon Hills Country Park
Essex (14 D5) **SS17 9NH**

Langley Park
Bucks (14 A5) **SL3 6DW**
Lanhydrock
Corn (3 H3) **PL30 5AD**
Leamington Spa Art
Gallery & Museum
Warks **CV32 4AA**
Lee Valley Park
Essex (14 C4) **EN9 1XQ**
Leeds Art Gallery
WYorks (24 A3) **LS1 3AA**
Leeds Castle & Gardens
Kent (9 E3) **ME17 1PL**
Legoland Windsor
W&M (14 A6) **SL4 4AY**
Lichfield Cathedral
Staffs **WS13 7LD**
Lickey Hills Country Park
Worcs (12 D1) **B45 8ER**
Lighthouse, The - Poole's
Centre for the Arts
Poole (6 D5) **BH15 1UG**
Lighthouse, The, Glasgow
Glas **G1 3NU**
Lightwater Valley Park
NYorks (24 A1) **HG4 3HT**
Linacre Reservoirs
Derbys (24 B6) **S42 7JW**
Lincoln Castle
Lincs **LN1 3AA**
Lincoln Cathedral
Lincs **LN2 1PL**
Liverpool Cathedral
Mersey **L1 7AZ**
Liverpool Metropolitan
Cathedral (RC) *Mersey* **L3 5TQ**
Living Coasts, Torquay
Torbay **TQ1 2BG**
Llandegfedd Reservoir
Mon (12 A5) **NP4 0TA**
Llanelli Millennium Coastal Park
Carmar (10 D4) **SA15 2LF**
Llangollen Railway
Denb (17 F3) **LL20 8SN**
Llechwedd Slate Caverns
Gwyn (16 D3) **LL41 3NB**
Llyn Brenig
Conwy (17 E3) **LL21 9TT**
Llyn Llech Owain Country Park
Carmar (11 E4) **SA14 7NF**
Llys-y-frân Reservoir Country Park
Pembs (10 B3) **SA63 4RR**
Loch an Eilein Visitor Centre &
Forest Trail
High (40 A5) **PH22 1QT**
Loch Lomond Shores &
Gateway Centre
WDun (31 G2) **G83 8QL**
Loch Ness Exhibition Centre
High (39 H4) **IV63 6TU**

Lochore Meadows Country Park
 Fife (32 C1) **KY5 8BA**
Locomotion: The National
 Railway Museum at
 Shildon *Dur* **DL4 1PQ**
Loggerheads Country Park
 Denb (22 B6) **CH7 5LH**
London Aquarium
 GtLon **SE1 7PD**
London Eye
 GtLon (14 C6) **SE1 7PB**
London Transport Museum
 GtLon **WC2E 7BB**
London Wetland Centre
 GtLon **SW13 9WT**
London Zoo
 GtLon **NW1 4RY**
Longleat House
 Wilts (6 C2) **BA12 7NW**
Longleat Safari Park
 Wilts (6 C2) **BA12 7NW**
Longniddry Bents
 ELoth (32 D2) **EH32 0PX**
Look Out Discovery Park,
 Bracknell
 BrackF (13 H6) **RG12 7QW**
Lord's Cricket Ground &
 Museum *GtLon* **NW8 8QN**
Lost Gardens of Heligan
 Corn (3 H4) **PL26 6EN**
Lotherton Hall Estate
 WYorks (24 B3) **LS25 3EB**
Loudoun Castle Park
 EAyr (31 H5) **KA4 8PE**
Louis Tussaud's Waxworks
 B'pool (22 C3) **FY1 5AA**
Lowry, The
 GtLon (23 E5) **M50 3AZ**
Lulworth Cove & Heritage Centre
 Dorset (6 C6) **BH20 5RQ**
Lunderston Bay
 Invcly (31 F3) **PA16 0DN**
Lynton & Lynmouth
 Cliff Railway
 Devon (5 E1) **EX35 6EP**

Madame Tussauds
 GtLon (14 B5) **NW1 5LR**
Magna Centre, Rotherham
 SYorks **S60 1DX**
Manchester Apollo
 GtMan **M12 6AP**
Manchester Art Gallery
 GtMan **M2 3JL**
Manchester Central
 GtMan (23 E5) **M2 3GX**
Manchester Craft &
 Design Centre *GtMan* **M4 5JD**
Manchester Museum
 GtMan **M13 9PL**

Manchester United Museum &
 Stadium Tour Centre
 GtMan **M16 0RA**
Mannings Amusement Park
 Suff (15 G3) **IP11 2DW**
Manor Farm Country Park
 Hants (7 F4) **SO30 2ER**
Marbury Country Park
 ChesW&C (22 D6) **CW9 6AT**
Margam Country Park
 NPT (11 F5) **SA13 2TJ**
Markeaton Park Craft Village
 Derby **DE22 3BG**
Market Bosworth Country Park
 Leics (19 E4) **CV13 0LP**
Marsh Farm Country Park
 Essex **CM3 5WP**
Marston Vale Millennium
 Country Park
 CenBeds (14 A2) **MK43 0PR**
Martin Mere
 Lancs (22 C4) **L40 0TA**
Marwell Zoo
 Hants (7 G3) **SO21 1JH**
Mary Rose
 Ports (7 G4) **PO1 3LX**
Mersey Ferries
 Mersey (22 C5) **CH44 6QY**
Merseyside Maritime Museum
 Mersey **L3 4AQ**
Mid Hants Railway
 Hants **SO24 9JG**
Midland Railway Centre
 Derbys **DE5 3QZ**
Mile End Park *GtLon* **E3 4HL**
Milky Way Adventure Park
 Devon **EX39 5RY**
Millennium Seed Bank,
 Wakehurst Place
 WSuss **RH17 6TN**
Milton Country Park
 Cambs **CB24 6AZ**
Minack Theatre *Corn* **TR19 6JU**
Modern Art Oxford
 Oxon **OX1 1BP**
Moel Famau Country Park
 Denb (22 B6) **LL15 1US**
Monikie Country Park
 Angus (37 E3) **DD5 3QN**
Monkey Mates
 W'ham **RG41 1JA**
Monkey World, Wareham
 Dorset (6 C5) **BH20 6HH**
Montacute House
 Som **TA15 6XP**
Montpellier Gallery,
 Stratford-upon-Avon
 Warks (13 E2) **CV37 6EP**
Moors Centre, Danby
 NYorks **YO21 2NB**

Moors Valley Country Park
 Dorset (7 E4) **BH24 2ET**
Moors Valley Railway
 Dorset **BH24 2ET**
Morden Hall Park
 GtLon **SM4 5JD**
Morwellham Quay Museum
 Devon **PL19 8JL**
Mother Shipton's Cave
 NYorks **HG5 8DD**
Mottisfont Abbey
 Hants **SO51 0LP**
Mount Edgcumbe Country Park
 Corn (4 C6) **PL10 1HZ**
Mugdock Country Park
 Stir (31 H3) **G62 8EL**
Muiravonside Country Park
 Falk (32 B2) **EH49 6LW**
Museum in Docklands
 GtLon **E14 4AL**
Museum of Childhood
 Edin **EH1 1TG**
Museum of Childhood
 GtLon **E2 9PA**
Museum of Flight
 ELoth **EH39 5LF**
Museum of Garden History,
 London *GtLon* **SE1 7LB**
Museum of London
 GtLon **EC2Y 5HN**
Museum of Science & Industry,
 Manchester
 GtMan (23 E5) **M3 4FP**
Museum of Transport
 Glas (31 H3) **G3 8DP**
Mustard Shop, Norwich
 Norf **NR2 1NQ**
M.V. Princess Pocahontas
 Kent (14 D6) **DA11 0BS**

National Agricultural Centre,
 Stoneleigh
 Warks (13 F1) **CV8 2LZ**
National Army Museum
 GtLon **SW3 4HT**
National Botanic Garden of Wales
 Carmar (11 E4) **SA32 8HG**
National Coal Mining Museum
 for England *WYorks* **WF4 4RH**
National Exhibition Centre
 WMid (18 D5) **B40 1NT**
National Fishing Heritage Centre,
 Grimsby *NELincs* **DN31 1UZ**
National Gallery
 GtLon (14 B5) **WC2N 5DN**
National Gallery of Scotland
 Edin (32 C2) **EH2 2EL**
National Indoor Arena,
 Birmingham
 WMid (18 C5) **B1 2AA**

National Library of Wales
Cere (16 C6) **SY23 3BU**
National Marine Aquarium
Plym (4 C6) **PL4 0LF**
National Maritime Museum
Cornwall *Corn* **TR11 3QY**
National Maritime Museum,
Greenwich *GtLon* **SE10 9NF**
National Media Museum,
Bradford
WYorks (24 A3) **BD1 1NQ**
National Memorial Arboretum,
Alrewas *Staffs* **DE13 7AR**
National Motorcycle Museum,
Solihull *WMid* (18 D5) **B92 0EJ**
National Museum Cardiff
Cardiff (11 H6) **CF10 3NP**
National Museum of Scotland
Edin (32 C2) **EH1 1JF**
National Portrait Gallery
GtLon **WC2H 0HE**
National Railway Museum
York (24 C2) **YO26 4XJ**
National Roman Legion
Museum, Caerleon
Newport (12 A5) **NP18 1AE**
National Sea Life Centre,
Birmingham
WMid (18 C5) **B1 2JB**
National Seal Sanctuary
Corn (3 G5) **TR12 6UG**
National Showcaves Centre for
Wales *Powys* (11 F4) **SA9 1GJ**
National Slate Museum, Llanberis
Gwyn (16 C3) **LL55 4TY**
National Space Centre
Leic (19 F4) **LE4 5NS**
National Wallace Monument
Stir **FK9 5LF**
National War Museum
Edin **EH1 2NG**
National Waterfront Museum
Swan (11 E5) **SA1 3RD**
National Wildflower Centre,
Liverpool *Mersey* **L16 3NA**
Natural History Museum at
Tring *Herts* **HP23 6AP**
Natural History Museum, London
GtLon (14 B6) **SW7 5BD**
Needham Lake
Suff (15 F2) **IP6 8NU**
Needles Pleasure Park
IoW (7 F5) **PO39 0JD**
Ness Botanic Gardens
ChesW&C **CH64 4AY**
New Lanark World Heritage Site
SLan (32 A3) **ML11 9DB**
New Palace & Adventureland,
New Brighton
Mersey **CH45 2JX**

New Walk Museum & Art Gallery
Leic **LE1 7EA**
New Walton Pier
Essex (15 G3) **CO14 8ES**
Newark Castle, Newark-on-Trent
Notts **NG24 1BG**
Newby Hall
NYorks **HG4 5AE**
Newmillerdam Country Park
WYorks (24 B4) **WF2 6QP**
Newport Museum & Art Gallery
Newport (12 A5) **NP20 1PA**
Newquay Zoo
Corn (3 G3) **TR7 2LZ**
Newstead Abbey
Notts **NG15 8NA**
Norfolk Lavender, Heacham
Norf **PE31 7JE**
Normanby Hall Country Park
NLincs **DN15 9HU**
North Bay Miniature Railway
NYorks **YO12 6PF**
North Norfolk Railway
Norf **NR26 8RA**
North Riding Forest Park
NYorks (29 G6) **YO18 7LT**
North Yorkshire Moors Railway
NYorks (29 G6) **YO18 7AJ**
Northam Burrows Country Park
Devon (4 C2) **EX39 1XR**
Northumbria Craft Centre,
Morpeth *N'umb* **NE61 1PD**
Norwich Castle Museum &
Art Gallery *Norf* **NR1 3JU**
Norwich Cathedral
Norf (21 F4) **NR1 4DH**
Nottingham Castle Museum &
Art Gallery
Nott (19 F3) **NG1 6EL**
Nova, Prestatyn
Denb (22 A5) **LL19 7EY**
Nowton Park
Suff (15 E1) **IP29 5LU**
Nymans *WSuss* **RH17 6EB**

O2, The *GtLon* **SE10 0BB**
Oakwell Hall & Country Park
WYorks **WF17 9LG**
Oakwood Leisure Park
Pembs (10 B4) **SA67 8DE**
Ocean Beach Amusement Park,
Rhyl *Denb* (22 A5) **LL18 1UL**
Oceanarium
Bourne (6 D5) **BH2 5AA**
Odds Farm Park
Bucks **HP10 0LX**
Ogden Water
WYorks (23 F3) **HX2 8YA**
Ogston Reservoir
Derbys (24 B6) **DE55 6EL**

Old Blacksmith's Shop,
Gretna Green
D&G (27 H2) **DG16 5DY**
Old Royal Naval College,
Greenwich *GtLon* **SE10 9LW**
Old Station, The, Tintern Parva
Mon (12 B4) **NP16 7NX**
Oldbury Court Estate
Bristol (12 B6) **BS16 2JH**
Olympia *GtLon* **W14 8UX**
Osborne House
IoW (7 G5) **PO32 6JX**
Osterley Park & House
GtLon **TW7 4RB**
Otterton Mill *Devon* **EX9 7HG**
Our Dynamic Earth
Edin (32 C2) **EH8 8AS**
Oxford Cathedral
Oxon (13 G4) **OX1 1AB**
Oxford Story *Oxon* **OX1 3AJ**
Oxford University Museum of
Natural History
Oxon (13 G4) **OX1 3PW**

Padarn Country Park
Gwyn (16 C2) **LL55 4TY**
Paignton & Dartmouth
Steam Railway
Torbay (5 E6) **TQ4 6AF**
Paignton Pier
Torbay (5 E5) **TQ4 6BW**
Paignton Zoo
Torbay (5 E6) **TQ4 7EU**
Palace of Holyroodhouse
Edin **EH8 8DX**
Palacerigg Country Park
NLan (32 A2) **G67 3HU**
Paradise Park, Newhaven
ESuss (8 C5) **BN9 0DH**
Paradise Wildlife Park,
Broxbourne
Herts (14 C4) **EN10 7QA**
Park Rose Pottery & Leisure Park
ERid (25 F1) **YO15 3QF**
Paultons Park
Hants (7 F4) **SO51 6AL**
Pavilion Gardens, Buxton
Derbys (23 F6) **SK17 6XN**
Pemberton's Chocolate Farm
Carmar (10 C3) **SA34 0EX**
Pembrey Country Park
Carmar (10 D4) **SA16 0EJ**
Pembroke Castle
Pembs (10 B4) **SA71 4LA**
Pennington Flash Country Park
GtMan (22 D5) **WN7 3PA**
Penrhyn Castle
Gwyn (16 C2) **LL57 4HN**
People's Palace & Winter
Gardens *Glas* **G40 1AT**

xiv

Philharmonic Hall, Liverpool
Mersey **L1 9BP**
Photographer's Gallery, The,
London *GtLon* **WC2H 7HY**
Piece Hall, Halifax
WYorks (23 F3) **HX1 1RE**
Pitt Rivers Museum
Oxon **OX1 3PP**
Plantasia *Swan (11 E5)* **SA1 2AL**
Pleasure Beach, Great Yarmouth
Norf (21 H4) **NR30 3EH**
Pleasure Island Theme Park
NELincs (25 G4) **DN35 0PL**
Pleasurewood Hills Theme Park
Suff (21 H5) **NR32 5DZ**
Plessey Woods Country Park
N'umb (28 D1) **NE22 6AN**
Plymouth Pavilions
Plym (4 C6) **PL1 3LF**
Polesden Lacey
Surr (8 B3) **RH5 6BD**
Polkemmet Country Park
WLoth (32 B2) **EH47 0AD**
Poole Pottery
Poole (6 D5) **BH15 1HJ**
Port Lympne Wild Animal Park
Kent **CT21 4PD**
Porthkerry Country Park
VGlam (11 G6) **CF62 3BY**
Portland Basin Museum
GtMan **OL7 0QA**
Portmeirion Village
Gwyn (16 C4) **LL48 6ET**
Portsmouth Guildhall
Ports **PO1 2AB**
Portsmouth Historic Dockyard
Ports (7 G4) **PO1 3LJ**
Potteries Museum & Art Gallery
Stoke **ST1 3DW**
Powderham Castle
Devon **EX6 8JQ**
Powis Castle & Garden
Powys (17 F5) **SY21 8RG**
Preston Guildhall
Lancs (22 D3) **PR1 1HT**
Prickly Ball Farm & Hedgehog
Hospital *Devon* **TQ12 6BZ**
Priory Country Park
Bed (14 A2) **MK41 9SH**
Provand's Lordship *Glas* **G4 0RH**
Pugneys Country Park
WYorks (24 B4) **WF2 7EQ**

Quarry Bank Mill & Styal Estate
ChesE **SK9 4LA**
Queen Elizabeth Country Park,
Petersfield
Hants (7 H4) **PO8 0QE**
Queen Elizabeth Hall
GtLon **SE1 8XX**

Queen Elizabeth II Conference
Centre *GtLon* **SW1P 3EE**
Queen Elizabeth II Country Park,
Ashington *N'umb* **NE63 9YF**
Queen's Gallery,
Buckingham Palace
GtLon **SW1A 1AA**
Queen's Hall *Edin* **EH8 9JG**
Queen's View Centre
P&K (36 B1) **PH16 5NR**
Queenswood Country Park
Here (12 A2) **HR6 0PY**

R.A.F. Museum, Cosford
Shrop **TF11 8UP**
R.A.F. Museum, Hendon
GtLon **NW9 5LL**
Rand Farm Park
Lincs **LN8 5NJ**
Ravenglass & Eskdale Railway
Cumb **CA18 1SW**
Real Mary King's Close, The
Edin **EH1 1PG**
Rheged - the Village in the Hill
Cumb (27 H4) **CA11 0DQ**
R.H.S. Garden Harlow Carr
NYorks (24 A2) **HG3 1QB**
R.H.S. Garden Rosemoor
Devon **EX38 8PH**
R.H.S. Garden Wisley
Surr (8 A3) **GU23 6QB**
Rhyl Sun Centre
Denb (22 A5) **LL18 3AQ**
River Link Boat Cruises
Devon (5 E6) **TQ6 9AJ**
Riverside Country Park
Med (15 E6) **ME7 2XH**
Riviera International Centre
Torbay (5 F5) **TQ2 5LZ**
Robin Hill Countryside
Adventure Park *IoW* **PO30 2NU**
Robinswood Hill Country Park
Glos (12 C4) **GL4 6SX**
Rochester Cathedral
Med **ME1 1SX**
Roman Baths & Pump Room, Bath
B&NESom (12 C6) **BA1 1LZ**
Romney, Hythe &
Dymchurch Railway
Kent **TN28 8PL**
Rosliston Forestry Centre
Derbys **DE12 8JX**
Rosslyn Chapel
Midlo (32 C2) **EH25 9PU**
Rother Valley Country Park
SYorks (24 B5) **S26 5PQ**
Rothiemurchus
High (40 B5) **PH22 1QH**
Royal Academy of Arts
GtLon **W1J 0BD**

Royal Albert Hall
GtLon **SW7 2AP**
Royal Albert Memorial
Museum & Art Gallery,
Exeter *Devon (5 F4)* **EX4 3RX**
Royal Armouries Museum, Leeds
WYorks (24 B3) **LS10 1LT**
Royal Bath & West Showground
Som (6 B3) **BA4 6QN**
Royal Botanic Garden
Edin (32 C2) **EH3 5LR**
Royal Botanic Gardens, Kew
GtLon **TW9 3AB**
Royal Centre
Nott (19 F2) **NG1 5ND**
Royal Festival Hall
GtLon **SE1 8XX**
Royal Highland Showground
Edin (32 C2) **EH28 8NB**
Royal Horticultural Halls
GtLon **SW1P 2PB**
Royal Hospital Chelsea
GtLon **SW3 4SR**
Royal Mews,
Buckingham Palace
GtLon **SW1W 0QH**
Royal Naval Museum
Ports (7 G4) **PO1 3NH**
Royal Observatory Greenwich
GtLon **SE10 8XJ**
Royal Opera House
GtLon **WC2E 9DD**
Royal Pavilion, Brighton
B&H (8 C5) **BN1 1EE**
Royal Scots Regimental
Museum, The *Edin* **EH1 2YT**
Royal Scottish Academy
Edin **EH2 2EL**
Royal Victoria Country Park
Hants (7 F4) **SO31 5GA**
Royal Welch Fusiliers
Regimental Museum
Gwyn (16 B2) **LL55 2AY**
Royal Yacht Britannia
Edin (32 C2) **EH6 6JJ**
Rudyard Lake
Staffs (18 C2) **ST13 8RT**
Rufford Country Park
Notts (24 C6) **NG22 9DF**
Rugby Football Union,
Twickenham *GtLon* **TW1 1DZ**
Ruthin Craft Centre
Denb (17 F3) **LL15 1BB**
Rutland Water
Rut (19 G4) **LE15 8QL**

St. Aidan's Winery
N'umb (33 H3) **TD15 2RX**
St. Albans Cathedral
Herts (14 B4) **AL1 1BY**

St. Andrew's & Blackfriars Halls,
Norwich *Norf* (21 F4) **NR3 1AU**

St. Botolph's Church, Boston
Lincs **PE21 6NP**

St. David's Hall
Cardiff (11 H6) **CF10 1AH**

St. Fagans National
History Museum
Cardiff (11 H6) **CF5 6XB**

St. George's Hall, Liverpool
Mersey **L1 1JJ**

St. Giles' Cathedral
Edin (32 C2) **EH1 1RE**

St. John the Baptist Church,
Cirencester *Glos* **GL7 2NX**

St. Lawrence's Church, Eyam
Derbys **S32 5QH**

St. Martin-in-the-Fields Church
GtLon **WC2N 4JH**

St. Mary Magdalene Chapel,
Sandringham *Norf* **PE35 6EH**

St. Mary the Virgin Church,
Holy Island *N'umb* **TD15 2RX**

St. Mary the Virgin Church,
Oxford *Oxon* (13 G4) **OX1 4AH**

St. Mary the Virgin Church, Rye
ESuss (9 F5) **TN31 7HE**

St. Mary's Church, Whitby
NYorks (29 H5) **YO22 4JT**

St. Michael's Church, Hathersage
Derbys **S32 1AJ**

St. Michael's Mount
Corn (3 F5) **TR17 0HT**

St. Mildred's Church,
Whippingham *IoW* **PO32 6LP**

St. Mungo Museum of Religious
Life & Art *Glas* **G4 0RH**

St. Mungo's Cathedral
Glas **G4 0QZ**

St. Paul's Cathedral, London
GtLon **EC4M 8AD**

St. Winwaloe's Church,
Gunwalloe *Corn* **TR12 7QE**

Salisbury Cathedral
Wilts (7 E3) **SP1 2EF**

Sally Lunn's House, Bath
B&NESom **BA1 1NX**

Saltburn's Inclined Tramway
R&C **TS12 1DP**

Saltwell Park, Gateshead
T&W (28 D2) **NE9 5AX**

Sandwell Park Farm
WMid **B71 4BG**

Sandwell Valley Country Park
WMid (18 C5) **B71 4BG**

Scarborough Sea Life &
Marine Sanctuary
NYorks (29 H6) **YO12 6RP**

Science Museum
GtLon (14 B6) **SW7 2DD**

Scolton Manor Country Park
Pembs (10 B3) **SA62 5QL**

Scotch Whisky Heritage Centre
Edin **EH1 2NE**

Scottish Exhibition &
Conference Centre (S.E.C.C.)
Glas (31 H3) **G3 8YW**

Scottish National Gallery of
Modern Art *Edin* **EH4 3DR**

Scottish National Portrait Gallery
Edin **EH2 1JD**

Scottish Parliament
Edin (32 C2) **EH99 1SP**

Scottish Seabird Centre,
North Berwick *ELoth* **EH39 4SS**

Scottish Wool Centre, Aberfoyle
Stir (31 H1) **FK8 3UQ**

Sea Life Centre, Blackpool
B'pool (22 C3) **FY1 5AA**

Sea Life Centre, Brighton
B&H (8 C5) **BN2 1TB**

Sea Life Centre, Great Yarmouth
Norf (21 H4) **NR30 3AH**

Sea Life Centre, Weymouth
Dorset (6 B5) **DT4 7SX**

Sea Life Sanctuary, Hunstanton
Norf **PE36 5BH**

Sea-Life Adventure
S'end **SS1 2ER**

SeaQuarium, Rhyl
Denb (22 A5) **LL18 3AF**

Seaton Tramway
Devon **EX12 2NQ**

Seized! Revenue & Customs
Uncovered *Mersey* **L3 4AQ**

Sellafield Visitors Centre
Cumb **CA20 1PG**

Serpentine Gallery
GtLon **W2 3XA**

Severn Valley Railway
Shrop (18 B5) **DY12 1BG**

Sewerby Hall & Gardens
ERid **YO15 1EA**

Shakespeare's Birthplace
Warks (13 E2) **CV37 6QW**

Shakespeare's Globe Theatre
GtLon **SE1 9DT**

Shanklin Chine *IoW* **PO37 6BW**

Sheffield Botanic Gardens
SYorks (24 B5) **S10 2LN**

Sheffield Park Garden
ESuss (8 C4) **TN22 3QX**

Shepreth Wildlife Park
Cambs **SG8 6PZ**

Sheringham Park
Norf (21 F2) **NR26 8TL**

Sherwood Forest Country Park
Notts (24 C6) **NG21 9HN**

Sherwood Forest Fun Park
Notts **NG21 9QA**

Sherwood Pines Forest Park
Notts (24 C6) **NG21 9JL**

Shipley Country Park
Derbys (19 E2) **DE75 7GX**

Shri Venkateswara (Balaji)
Temple of the United
Kingdom *WMid* **B69 3DU**

Shrine of Our Lady of
Walsingham (Anglican)
Norf **NR22 6EF**

Shugborough Estate
Staffs **ST17 0XB**

Sirhowy Valley Country Park
Caerp (11 H5) **NP11 7BD**

Sissinghurst Castle Garden
Kent **TN17 2AB**

Skegness Natureland Seal
Sanctuary *Lincs* **PE25 1DB**

Skegness Water Leisure Park
Lincs (25 H6) **PE25 1JF**

Sky Tower, Rhyl
Denb (22 A5) **LL18 3AQ**

Slimbridge Wildfowl & Wetlands
Trust *Glos* (12 C4) **GL2 7BT**

Slipper Chapel, Houghton St. Giles
Norf **NR22 6AL**

Smugglers Adventure, Hastings
ESuss **TN34 3HY**

Snowdon Mountain Railway
Gwyn (16 C3) **LL55 4TY**

Snowshill Manor *Glos* **WR12 7JU**

Somerset House
GtLon **WC2R 1LA**

South Lakes Wild Animal Park
Cumb (22 B1) **LA15 8JR**

South Shields Museum &
Art Gallery
T&W (29 E2) **NE33 2JA**

Southend Pier
S'end (15 E5) **SS1 1EE**

Southport Pier *Mersey* **PR8 1QX**

Southwark Cathedral
GtLon **SE1 9DA**

Southwell Minster
Notts **NG25 0HD**

Spa Complex, Scarborough
NYorks **YO11 2HD**

Spean Bridge Woollen Mill
High (39 F6) **PH34 4EP**

Spinnaker Tower
Ports **PO1 3TN**

Spitfire & Hurricane Memorial,
R.A.F. Manston
Kent (15 H6) **CT12 5DF**

Stanborough Park
Herts (14 B4) **AL8 6XF**

Standalone Farm, Letchworth
Garden City *Herts* **SG6 4JN**

Standedge Tunnel & Visitor
Centre *WYorks* **HD7 6NQ**

Stapeley Water Gardens
ChesE (18 A2) **CW5 7LH**
Staunton Harold Reservoir
Derbys (19 E3) **DE73 8DN**
Stewart Park
Middl (29 F5) **TS7 8AR**
Stirling Castle
Stir (32 A1) **FK8 1EJ**
Stirling Visitor Centre
Stir **FK8 1EH**
Stockgrove Country Park
CenBeds (14 A3) **LU7 0BA**
Stonehenge
Wilts (7 E2) **SP4 7DE**
Stonham Barns
Suff (15 G2) **IP14 6AT**
Storybook Glen
Aber **AB12 5FT**
Stourhead
Wilts (6 C3) **BA12 6QD**
Stowe Landscape Gardens
Bucks **MK18 5DQ**
Stratford-upon-Avon Butterfly
Farm *Warks* **CV37 7LS**
Strathclyde Country Park
NLan (32 A3) **ML1 3ED**
Strinesdale Countryside Area
GtMan **OL4 2JJ**
Stuart & Waterford Crystal
Factory Shop, Crieff
P&K (36 B3) **PH7 4HQ**
Stuart Line Cruises, Exmouth
Devon (5 F4) **EX8 1EJ**
Studland & Godlington
Heath NNR
Dorset (6 D5) **BH19 3AX**
Studley Royal Park & ruins of
Fountains Abbey
NYorks (24 A1) **HG4 3DY**
Sudbury Hall *Derbys* **DE6 5HT**
Sunderland Museum &
Winter Gardens
T&W (29 E3) **SR1 1PP**
Sundown Adventure Land
Notts (24 D6) **DN22 0HX**
Sutton Bank National Park Centre
NYorks **YO7 2EH**
Swallow Falls
Conwy (16 D3) **LL24 0DW**
Swanage Railway
Dorset (6 D6) **BH19 1HB**
Swansea Museum
Swan (11 E5) **SA1 1SN**
Sywell Country Park
N'hants **NN6 0QX**

Talkin Tarn Country Park
Cumb (28 A3) **CA8 1HN**
Tank Museum, Bovington
Dorset **BH20 6JG**

Tate Britain
GtLon (14 C6) **SW1P 4RG**
Tate Liverpool
Mersey (22 C5) **L3 4BB**
Tate Modern
GtLon (14 C5) **SE1 9TG**
Tate St. Ives
Corn (3 F4) **TR26 1TG**
Tatton Park
ChesE (23 E5) **WA16 6QN**
Techniquest *Cardiff* **CF10 5BW**
Tehidy Country Park
Corn (3 F4) **TR14 0HA**
Telford Wonderland
Tel&W **TF3 4AY**
Temple Newsam
WYorks (24 B3) **LS15 0AE**
Teviot Water Gardens
ScBord (33 F4) **TD5 8LE**
Tewkesbury Abbey
Glos (12 C3) **GL20 5RZ**
Thermae Bath Spa
B&NESom **BA1 1SJ**
Thetford Forest Park
Norf (20 D5) **IP27 0TJ**
Thorndon Country Park
Essex (14 D5) **CM13 3RZ**
Thorpe Park
Surr (14 A6) **KT16 8PN**
Three Counties Showground
Worcs (12 C2) **WR13 6NW**
Thrybergh Country Park
SYorks (24 B5) **S65 4NU**
Thursford Collection
Norf **NR21 0AS**
Tilgate Park
WSuss (8 B4) **RH10 5PQ**
Tintagel Castle
Corn (3 H2) **PL34 0HE**
Tintern Abbey
Mon (12 B5) **NP16 6SE**
Tiptree Museum
Essex **CO5 0RF**
Titchwell Marsh *Norf* **PE31 8BB**
Tittesworth Reservoir &
Visitor Centre
Staffs (18 C2) **ST13 8TQ**
Tower Bridge Exhibition
GtLon **SE1 2UP**
Tower of London
GtLon (14 C5) **EC3N 4AB**
Towneley Hall Art Gallery &
Museum *Lancs* **BB11 3RQ**
Trago Mills, Newton Abbot
Devon (5 E5) **TQ12 6JD**
Trebah Garden *Corn* **TR11 5JZ**
Trelissick *Corn* **TR3 6QL**
Tropical Butterfly House,
Wildlife & Falconry Centre
SYorks **S25 4EQ**

Tropical World, Roundhay
WYorks (24 B3) **LS8 2ER**
Truro Cathedral
Corn (3 G4) **TR1 2AF**
Tulleys Farm
WSuss (8 C4) **RH10 4PE**
Tullibardine Distillery
P&K (36 C4) **PH4 1QG**
Tullie House Museum & Art
Gallery *Cumb* (27 H3) **CA3 8TP**
Tutankhamun Exhibition,
Dorchester
Dorset (6 B5) **DT1 1UW**
Tutbury Castle *Staffs* **DE13 9JF**
Twycross Zoo
Leics (19 E4) **CV9 3PX**
Tyne Green Country Park
N'umb **NE46 3RY**

Ulley Reservoir Country Park
SYorks (24 B5) **S26 3XL**
Ullswater Steamers
Cumb (27 H5) **CA11 0US**
University of Glasgow
Visitor Centre *Glas* **G12 8QQ**
Upper Derwent Reservoirs
Derbys (24 A5) **S33 0AQ**
Upton Country Park
Poole **BH17 7BJ**
Urbis, Manchester
GtMan **M4 3BG**
Urquhart Castle
High (39 H4) **IV63 6XJ**
Usher Hall *Edin* **EH1 2EA**

Ventnor Botanic Gardens
IoW (7 G6) **PO38 1UL**
Venue Cymru, Llandudno
Conwy (16 D1) **LL30 1BB**
Victoria & Albert Museum
GtLon (14 B6) **SW7 2RL**
Vogrie Country Park
MidLo (32 D2) **EH23 4NU**
Voirrey Embroidery
Mersey (22 C5) **CH63 6JA**
Volks Electric Railway
B&H **BN2 1EN**

Waddesdon Manor
Bucks (13 H4) **HP18 0JH**
Wakehurst Place
WSuss (8 C4) **RH17 6TN**
Wales Millennium Centre
Cardiff (11 H6) **CF10 5AL**
Walker Art Gallery, Liverpool
Mersey **L3 8EL**
Wallace Collection, London
GtLon **W1U 3BN**
Walsall Arboretum Illuminations
WMid (18 C5) **WS1 2AB**

Walton Hall Gardens *Warr (22 D5)* **WA4 6SN**

Wansbeck Riverside Park *N'umb* **NE63 8TX**

Warwick Castle *Warks (13 E1)* **CV34 4QU**

Waseley Hills Country Park *Worcs* **B45 9AT**

Wat Tyler Country Park *Essex* **SS16 4UH**

Watermead Country Park *Leics* **LE7 4PF**

Watermouth Castle *Devon* **EX34 9SL**

Waterperry *Oxon (13 G4)* **OX33 1JZ**

Watershed Mill Visitor Centre, Settle *NYorks (23 E1)* **BD24 9LR**

Watersmeet House *Devon* **EX35 6NT**

Waterworld, Hanley *Stoke (18 B2)* **ST1 5PU**

Weald & Downland Open Air Museum *WSuss* **PO18 0EU**

Weald Country Park *Essex (14 D5)* **CM14 5QS**

Wells Cathedral *Som (6 B2)* **BA5 2UE**

Welsh Mountain Zoo *Conwy (16 D2)* **LL28 5UY**

Wembley *GtLon (14 B5)* **HA9 0WS**

Wensleydale Cheese Visitor Centre, Hawes *NYorks (28 B6)* **DL8 3RN**

Wepre Country Park *Flints (22 B6)* **CH5 4HL**

West Midland Safari Park & Leisure Park *Worcs (12 C1)* **DY12 1LF**

West Somerset Railway *Som (5 G2)* **TA24 5BG**

West Stow Country Park *Suff (15 E1)* **IP28 6HG**

Westminster Abbey *GtLon* **SW1P 3PA**

Westminster Abbey - Chapter House & Pyx Chamber *GtLon* **SW1P 3PA**

Westminster Cathedral *GtLon* **SW1P 2QW**

Weston Park *Staffs (18 B4)* **TF11 8LE**

Westonbirt - The National Arboretum *Glos (12 C5)* **GL8 8QS**

Westpoint Arena, Clyst St. Mary *Devon (5 F4)* **EX5 1DJ**

Whinlatter Forest *Cumb* **CA12 5TW**

Whipsnade Zoo *CenBeds (14 A4)* **LU6 2LF**

Whitby Abbey *NYorks* **YO22 4JT**

Whitby Lifeboat Museum *NYorks* **YO21 3PU**

White Cube *GtLon* **N1 6PB**

White Post Farm Centre, Farnsfield *Notts (19 F2)* **NG22 8HL**

Whitworth Art Gallery, Manchester *GtMan* **M15 6ER**

Wicksteed Park *N'hants (13 H1)* **NN15 6NJ**

Wigan Pier *GtMan* **WN3 4EU**

Willen Lakeside Park *MK (13 H3)* **MK15 9HQ**

Willows Farm Village *Herts (14 B4)* **AL2 1BB**

Wilton House *Wilts* **SP2 0BJ**

Wimbledon All England Lawn Tennis & Croquet Club *GtLon* **SW19 5AG**

Wimborne Minster *Dorset* **BH21 1HT**

Wimpole Home Farm *Cambs (14 C2)* **SG8 0BW**

Winchester Cathedral *Hants (7 F3)* **SO23 9LS**

Windermere Lake Cruises *Cumb (27 H6)* **LA12 8AS**

Windsor Castle *W&M (14 A6)* **SL4 1NJ**

Winter Gardens, Blackpool *B'pool (22 C3)* **FY1 1HW**

Winter Gardens, Weston-super-Mare *NSom (12 A6)* **BS23 1AJ**

Wirral Country Park *Mersey (22 B5)* **CH61 0HN**

Woburn Safari Park *CenBeds (14 A3)* **MK17 9QN**

Wolds Village, Bainton *ERid* **YO25 9EF**

Wolverhampton Art Gallery *WMid* **WV1 1DU**

Wood Green Animal Shelter, Godmanchester *Cambs (14 B1)* **PE29 2NH**

Woodlands Leisure Park, Dartmouth *Devon (5 E6)* **TQ9 7DQ**

Woodside Animal Farm & Leisure Park *CenBeds* **LU1 4DG**

Wookey Hole Caves & Papermill *Som (6 B2)* **BA5 1BB**

Worcester Cathedral *Worcs* **WR1 2LH**

Worcester Woods Country Park *Worcs (12 C2)* **WR5 2LG**

World Museum Liverpool *Mersey (22 C5)* **L3 8EN**

World of Beatrix Potter Attraction *Cumb (27 H6)* **LA23 3BX**

World of James Herriot, Thirsk *NYorks* **YO7 1PL**

W.R. Outhwaite & Son Ropemakers *NYorks* **DL8 3NT**

Wrexham Arts Centre *Wrex (17 G3)* **LL11 1AU**

Wroxham Barns *Norf (21 G3)* **NR12 8QU**

Wycoller Country Park *Lancs* **BB8 8SY**

Wynyard Woodland Park *Stock* **TS21 3JG**

Wyre Forest *Worcs (12 C1)* **DY14 9XQ**

Xscape Castleford *WYorks (24 B3)* **WF10 4DA**

Ye Olde Pork Pie Shoppe, Melton Mowbray *Leics (19 G4)* **LE13 1NW**

Yellowcraig *ELoth (33 E1)* **EH39 5DS**

Yeovil Country Park *Som (6 B4)* **BA20 1QZ**

York Castle Museum *York (24 C2)* **YO1 9SA**

York Dungeon *York* **YO1 9RD**

York Minster *York (24 C2)* **YO1 7HH**

Yorkshire Sculpture Park *WYorks (24 A4)* **WF4 4LG**

Airports

Each of the following airports are shown on the map within this atlas. The map reference is shown in brackets after the name of the airport e.g. Aberdeen Airport is on page 41 in grid square F5.

Aberdeen (41 F5)	**AB21 7DU**	Inverness (40 A3)	**IV2 7JB**
Alderney (5 H5)	**GY9 3XD**	Islay (30 B4)	**PA42 7AS**
Barra (44 A9)	**HS9 5YA**	Isle of Man (26 B6)	**IM9 2AS**
Benbecula (44 B7)	**HS7 5LA**	Jersey (5 G6)	**JE1 1BY**
Birmingham International (18 D5)	**B26 3QJ**	Kent International (15 H6)	**CT12 5BL**
Blackpool International (22 C3)	**FY4 2QY**	Kirkwall (45 C3)	**KW15 1TH**
Bournemouth (7 E5)	**BH23 6SE**	Leeds Bradford International (24 A2)	**LS19 7TU**
Bristol Filton (12 B5)	**BS99 7AR**	Liverpool John Lennon (22 C5)	**L24 1YD**
Bristol International (12 B6)	**BS48 3DY**	London Ashford (9 F4)	**TN29 9QL**
Campbeltown (30 C5)	**PA28 6NU**	Luton (14 B4)	**LU2 9LY**
Cardiff International (11 G6)	**CF62 3BD**	Manchester (23 E5)	**M90 1QX**
City (14 C5)	**E16 2PX**	Newcastle International (28 D2)	**NE13 8BZ**
Coventry (13 F1)	**CV3 4PB**	Newquay Cornwall International (3 G3)	**TR8 4RQ**
Dundee (37 E3)	**DD2 1UH**	Norwich International (21 F4)	**NR6 6JA**
Durham Tees Valley (29 E5)	**DL2 1LU**	Plymouth City (4 D6)	**PL6 8BW**
East Midlands (19 E3)	**DE74 2SA**	Robin Hood Doncaster Sheffield (24 C5)	**DN9 3RH**
Edinburgh (32 C2)	**EH12 9DN**	Shoreham (8 B5)	**BN43 5FF**
Exeter International (5 F4)	**EX5 2BD**	Southampton (7 F4)	**SO18 2NL**
Gatwick (8 B3)	**RH6 0NP**	Southend (15 E5)	**SS2 6YF**
Glasgow (31 G3)	**PA3 2SW**	Stansted (14 D3)	**CM24 1QW**
Glasgow Prestwick (31 G5)	**KA9 2PL**	Stornoway (44 E3)	**HS2 0BN**
Guernsey (5 G5)	**GY8 0DS**	Sumburgh (45 H6)	**ZE3 9JP**
Heathrow (14 A6)	**UB3 5AP**	Tiree (34 A2)	**PA77 6TN**
Humberside (25 E4)	**DN39 6YH**	Wick (43 H3)	**KW1 4QP**

Ferry terminals

Aberdeen to Kirkwall, NorthLink Ferries	**AB11 5NP**	Holyhead to Dublin, Stena Line	**LL65 1DQ**
Aberdeen to Lerwick, NorthLink Ferries	**AB11 5NP**	Holyhead to Dun Laoghaire, Stena Line	**LL65 1DQ**
Ardrossan to Brodick, Caledonian MacBrayne	**KA22 8ED**	Kennacraig to Colonsay, Caledonian MacBrayne	**PA29 6YF**
Birkenhead to Belfast, Norfolk Line Ferries	**CH41 1FE**	Kennacraig to Port Askaig, Caledonian MacBrayne	**PA29 6YF**
Birkenhead to Dublin, Norfolk Line Ferries	**CH41 1FE**	Kennacraig to Port Ellen, Caledonian MacBrayne	**PA29 6YF**
Cairnryan to Larne, P&O Irish Sea	**DG9 8RF**	Kingston upon Hull to Rotterdam, P&O Ferries	**HU9 5PR**
Claonaig to Lochranza, Caledonian MacBrayne	**PA29 6YG**	Kingston upon Hull to Zeebrugge, P&O Ferries	**HU9 5PR**
Dover to Boulogne, L D Lines	**CT16 1JA**	Lerwick to Kirkwall, NorthLink Ferries	**ZE1 0PW**
Dover to Calais, P&O Ferries	**CT16 1JA**	Liverpool to Douglas, Isle of Man Steam Packet Co.	**L3 1DL**
Dover to Calais, SeaFrance	**CT16 3PX**	Liverpool to Dublin, P&O Irish Sea	**L20 1BG**
Dover to Dieppe, L D Lines	**CT16 1JA**	Lymington to Yarmouth, Wightlink	**SO41 5SB**
Dover to Dunkerque, Norfolk Line Ferries	**CT16 1JA**	Mallaig to Armadale, Caledonian MacBrayne	**PH41 4QD**
Fishguard to Rosslare, Stena Line	**SA64 0BU**	Newcastle upon Tyne to Amsterdam, DFDS Seaways	**NE29 6EE**
Fleetwood to Larne, Stena Line	**FY7 6HP**	Newhaven to Dieppe, Transmanche Ferries	**BN9 0DF**
Gill's Bay to St. Margaret's Hope, Pentland Ferries	**KW1 4YB**	Oban to Castlebay, Caledonian MacBrayne	**PA34 4DB**
Harwich to Esbjerg, DFDS Seaways	**CO12 4QG**	Oban to Coll, Caledonian MacBrayne	**PA34 4DB**
Harwich to Hook of Holland, Stena Line	**CO12 4SR**	Oban to Colonsay, Caledonian MacBrayne	**PA34 4DB**
Heysham to Douglas, Isle of Man Steam Packet Co.	**LA3 2XF**		
Holyhead to Dublin, Irish Ferries	**LL65 1DR**		

Oban to Craignure, Caledonian MacBrayne		**PA34 4DB**
Oban to Lismore, Caledonian MacBrayne		**PA34 4DB**
Oban to Lochboisdale, Caledonian MacBrayne		**PA34 4DB**
Oban to Tiree, Caledonian MacBrayne		**PA34 4DB**
Pembroke to Rosslare, Irish Ferries		**SA72 6UF**
Penzance to St. Mary's, Isle of Scilly Steamship Co.		**TR18 4BD**
Plymouth to Roscoff, Brittany Ferries		**PL1 3EW**
Plymouth to Santander, Brittany Ferries		**PL1 3EW**
Poole to Channel Islands & St. Malo, Condor Ferries		**BH15 4AJ**
Poole to Cherbourg, Brittany Ferries		**BH15 4AJ**
Portsmouth to Bilbao, P&O Ferries		**PO2 8QN**
Portsmouth to Caen, Brittany Ferries		**PO2 8RU**
Portsmouth to Channel Islands, Condor Ferries		**PO2 8SP**
Portsmouth to Cherbourg, Brittany Ferries		**PO2 8RU**
Portsmouth to Cherbourg, Condor Ferries		**PO2 8SP**
Portsmouth to Fishbourne, Wightlink		**PO1 3PS**
Portsmouth to Le Havre, L D Lines		**PO2 8QN**
Portsmouth to St. Malo, Brittany Ferries		**PO2 8RU**
Portsmouth to Santander, Brittany Ferries		**PO2 8RU**
Rosyth to Zeebrugge, Norfolk Line Ferries		**KY11 2XP**
Scrabster to Stromness, NorthLink Ferries		**KW14 7UT**
Southampton to East Cowes, Red Funnel Ferries		**SO14 2AQ**
Stranraer to Belfast, Stena Line		**DG9 7RD**
Tarbert to Lochranza, Caledonian MacBrayne		**HS3 3DG**
Troon to Larne, P&O Irish Sea		**KA10 6HH**
Uig to Lochmaddy, Caledonian MacBrayne		**IV51 9XX**
Uig to Tarbert, Caledonian MacBrayne		**IV51 9XX**
Ullapool to Stornoway, Caledonian MacBrayne		**IV26 2UR**
Weymouth to Channel Islands & St. Malo, Condor Ferries		**DT4 8DX**

Channel Tunnel

Eurostar		
Ashford International		**TN24 0PS**
Ebbsfleet International		**DA10 1EB**
St. Pancras International		**NW1 2TB**
EuroTunnel		
Folkestone		**CT18 8XX**

Park and Rides

Many towns and cities now operate Park and Ride services which mean visitors can park their car in a secure out-of-town car park and catch a frequent bus, tram or train service into the centre. Park and Ride services are listed below by town. Choose the service you require based on the direction of your approach to the town. Enter the full postcode into your Sat Nav. In the example below if you are travelling to Bristol on the M5 the best Park and Ride service to use is Portway so enter the postcode **BS11 9QE** into your Sat Nav.

Bristol			
Bath Road	East		**BS4 5LR**
Long Ashton	South and West		**BS3 2HB**
Portway	M5		**BS11 9QE**

Aberdeen			
Bridge of Don	North		**AB23 8BL**
Ellon	North		**AB41 9RY**
Kingswells	West		**AB15 8PJ**
Aberystwyth			**SY23 1PH**
Barnstaple			**EX32 9AX**
Bath			
Lansdown	North		**BA1 9BJ**
Newbridge	West		**BA1 3NB**
Bath			
Odd Down	South		**BA2 8PA**
Bedford			
Elstow			**MK42 9XF**
Birmingham			
Black Lake	North West		**B70 0NR**
Blake Street	North		**B74 4YD**
Hawthorns, The	North West		**B66 2HB**
Priestfield	North West		**WV2 2NN**
Selly Oak	South		**B29 6AA**

Birmingham		
Stourbridge Junction	West	**DY8 1NH**
Sutton Coldfield	North	**B73 6AY**
Wednesbury Parkway		**WS10 7WJ**
Brighton		
Withdean		**BN1 5JD**
Bristol		
Bath Road	East	**BS4 5LR**
Long Ashton	South and West	**BS3 2HB**
Portway	M5	**BS11 9QE**
Brixham		**TQ5 0JT**
Cambridge		
Babraham Road	South and South East	**CB22 3AB**
Madingley Road	West and North West	**CB3 0EX**
Milton	North	**CB24 6DQ**
Newmarket Road	East	**CB5 8AA**
Trumpington Road	South	**CB2 9FT**
Canterbury		
New Dover	South East	**CT1 3EJ**
Sturry Road	North East	**CT2 0AA**
Wincheap	West	**CT1 3TY**
Cardiff		
Ebbw Vale Parkway	North	**NP23 8AP**
Llanhilleth	North	**NP13 2JA**
Chelmsford		**CM2 7RU**
Cheltenham		
Arle Court	West and M5	**GL51 6TA**
Racecourse	North and East	**GL50 4SH**
Chester		
Boughton Heath	South and East	**CH3 5QD**
Sealand Road	West	**CH1 4LD**
Upton (The Zoo)	North	**CH2 1LH**
Wrexham Road	South and West	**CH4 7QR**
Coventry		
North	North	**CV6 7NS**
South	South	**CV3 6PH**
Cowes		**PO31 8HU**
Dartmouth		**TQ6 9LW**
Derby		
Meteor Centre	North	**DE21 4SY**
Pride Park	South and East	**DE24 8AN**

Doncaster		
Doncaster North	North and West	**DN5 7UN**
Doncaster South	South and West	**DN11 0GT**
Durham		
Belmont	East and A1(M)	**DH1 1SR**
Howlands Farm	South	**DH1 3TQ**
Sniperly	North and West	**DH1 5AB**
Edinburgh		
Ferrytoll	North	**KY11 1LL**
Hermiston	West	**EH14 5PX**
Ingliston	West	**EH28 8LS**
Newcraighall	East	**EH21 6TT**
Sherrifhall	South East	**EH22 1FF**
Straiton	South	**EH20 9NP**
Wallyford	East	**EH21 8BU**
Exeter		
Honiton Road	North and East	**EX1 3RU**
Matford	South and West	**EX2 8ED**
Sowton	South East	**EX2 7JH**
Falkirk		**FK1 4JQ**
Falmouth		**TR11 2SG**
Glasgow		
Chatelherault	South East	**ML3 7UB**
Dalmuir	North and North West	**G81 3QT**
Greenfaulds	North East	**G67 2XJ**
Shields Road	South	**G5 8QF**
Gloucester		
St. Oswalds Park	North, East and West	**GL1 2SG**
Waterwells	South	**GL2 2AN**
Guernsey		**GY1 2UL**
Guildford		
Artington	South	**GU3 1LP**
Merrow	East	**GU4 7AA**
Spectrum	North	**GU1 1UP**
High Wycombe		**HP11 1UA**
Horsham		**RH13 0AR**
Ipswich		
Bury Road	North	**IP1 5QL**
London Road	South and West	**IP8 3TQ**
Martlesham Heath	East	**IP5 3QX**
Kingston upon Hull		
Priory Park	South and West	**HU4 7DY**
Walton Street		**HU3 6JR**

Leicester		
Enderby	South and West	**LE19 2BX**
Meynells Grove	North and West	**LE3 3LF**
Liverpool		
Lea Green	East	**WA9 5AF**
St. Helens Junction	East	**WA9 3LA**
Shotton	South	**CH5 1BX**
Ludlow		**SY8 1FD**
Maidstone		
London Road	West	**ME16 0LP**
Sittingbourne Road	North and M20	**ME14 3EN**
Willington Street	East	**ME15 8JW**
Manchester		
Ladywell Tram		**M6 8HD**
Whitefield		**M45 8QH**
Milton Keynes		**MK16 0AA**
Newcastle upon Tyne		
Callerton Parkway	North West	**NE13 8BP**
Four Lane Ends	North	**NE7 7UH**
Heworth		
Interchange	South	**NE10 0NT**
Kingston Park	North and West	**NE3 2SW**
Regent Centre	North	**NE3 3JN**
Norwich		
Airport	North	**NR6 6JT**
Costessy	West	**NR9 3LX**
Harford	South	**NR4 6DY**
Postwick	East	**NR13 5NP**
Sprowston	North	**NR7 8RN**
Thickthorn	South West	**NR9 3AU**
Nottingham		
Forest, The	West	**NG7 6ND**
Hucknall	North	**NG15 7UQ**
Moor Bridge	North	**NG6 8AB**
Parkway	South West	**NG11 0EB**
Phoenix Park	West	**NG8 6AR**
Queens Drive	South and West	**NG2 1RS**
Racecourse, The	East	**NG2 4BE**
Wilkinson Street	West	**NG7 7NU**
Oxford		
Peartree	North and West	**OX2 8JD**
Redbridge	South	**OX1 4YG**
Seacourt	South West	**OX2 0HP**
Thornhill	East	**OX3 8DP**
Water Eaton	North	**OX2 8HA**
Perth		
Perth	South, North and West	**PH1 1RA**
Scone	East	**PH2 6RD**

Plymouth		
Coypool	East	**PL7 4NW**
George Junction	North	**PL6 7HB**
Ivybridge	East	**PL21 0DQ**
Milehouse	West	**PL2 3DQ**
Preston		
Portway	South and West	**PR1 8PQ**
Walton-le-dale	South and East	**PR5 4AW**
Reading		
Loddon Bridge	East	**RG41 5HG**
Madejski Stadium	South, West on M4	**RG2 0FL**
Ryde		**PO33 2BA**
Salisbury		
Beehive	North	**SP4 6BQ**
Britford	South	**SP5 4DS**
London Road	North and East	**SP1 3JB**
Wilton	West	**SP2 0AG**
Scarborough		
Filey Road	South East	**YO11 3JY**
Seamer Road	South West	**YO12 4LW**
Sheffield		
Halfway	South and South East	**S20 3GS**
Malin Bridge	West and North West	**S6 4JR**
Meadowhall Interchange	M1	**S9 1EP**
Middlewood	West and North West	**S6 1TQ**
Nunnery Square	East	**S2 5BD**
Shrewsbury		
Harlescott	North and East	**SY1 4AB**
Meole Brace	South	**SY3 8NB**
Oxon	West	**SY3 5AH**
Solihull		**B91 3LU**
Southport		
Espanlade	South	**PR1 1RX**
Fairways	North	**PR9 0LA**
Kew	South East	**PR9 7RG**
Stirling		
Castleview	West and M9	**FK9 4TW**
Springkerse	East	**FK7 7TL**
Stratford		**CV37 0RW**
Swansea		
Fabian Way	East	**SA1 8LD**
Fforestfach	North West	**SA5 4EE**
Landore	North	**SA1 2JT**

Swindon		
Groundwell	North	**SN2 5LX**
Wroughton	South	**SN3 1TA**
Taunton		
Silk Mills	West	**TA1 5AA**
Taunton East	East and M5	**TA3 5LU**
Truro		**TR4 9AN**
Winchester		**SO23 9SQ**
Worcester		**WR3 7NS**

York		
Askham Bar	South West	**YO24 1LW**
Designer Outlet	South	**YO19 4TA**
Grimston Bar	East	**YO19 5LA**
Monks Cross	North East	**YO32 9JU**
Rawcliffe Bar	North West	**YO30 5XZ**

National and Forest Parks

Afan Forest Park	
Afan Forest Park Visitor Centre	**SA13 3HG**
Argyll Forest Park	
Ardgarten Visitor Centre	**G83 7AR**
Brecon Beacons National Park	
Abergavenny Tourist Information and	
National Park Centre	**NP7 5HL**
Brecon Beacons National Park	
Visitor Centre	**LD3 8ER**
Craig-y-Nos Country Park	
Visitor Centre	**SA9 1GL**
Llandovery Tourist Information and	
Heritage Centre	**SA20 0AW**
Waterfalls Centre	**SA11 5NR**
Cairngorms National Park	
Aviemore Tourist Information Centre	**PH22 1RH**
Coed y Brenin Forest Park	
Coed y Brenin Visitor Centre	**LL40 2HZ**
Dartmoor National Park	
Haytor Information Centre	**TQ13 9XT**
High Moorland Visitor Centre	**PL20 6QF**
Postbridge National Park	
Information Centre	**PL20 6TH**
Dean Forest and Wye Valley Forest Park	
Beechenhurst Lodge	**GL16 7EG**
Cannop Cycle Centre	**GL16 7EH**
Delamere Forest Park	
Linmere Visitor Centre	**CW8 2JD**
Exmoor National Park	
Exmoor National Park Centre,	
Dulverton	**TA22 9EX**
Exmoor National Park Centre,	
Dunster	**TA24 6SE**

Exmoor National Park Centre,	
Lynmouth	**EX35 6NY**
Galloway Forest Park	
Clatteringshaws Visitor Centre	**DG7 3SQ**
Glentrool Visitor Centre	**DG8 6SU**
Kirroughtree Visitor Centre	**DG8 7BE**
Glenmore Forest Park	
Visitor Centre	**PH22 1QU**
Grizedale Forest Park	
Visitor Centre	**LA22 0QJ**
Gwydyr Forest Park	
Visitor Centre	**LL26 0PN**
Kielder Forest Park	
Kielder Castle Forest Park Centre	**NE48 1ER**
Lake District National Park	
Lake District Visitor Centre at	
Brockhole	**LA23 1LJ**
Loch Lomond and Trossachs	
National Park	
National Park Centre, Balmaha	**G63 0JQ**
National Park Centre, Luss	**G83 8PA**
National Park Gateway Centre,	
Loch Lomond Shores	**G83 8QL**
New Forest National Park	
New Forest Museum and	
Information Centre	**SO43 7NY**
North Riding Forest Park	
Dalby Forest Visitor Centre	**YO18 7LT**
North York Moors National Park	
Moors Centre, The	**YO21 2NB**
Old Coastguard Station	**YO22 4SJ**
Sutton Bank	**YO7 2EH**

Northumberland National Park	
National Park Centre, Ingram	**NE66 4LT**
National Park Centre, Once Brewed	**NE47 7AN**
National Park Centre, Rothbury	**NE65 7UP**
Peak District National Park	
Bakewell Visitor Centre	**DE45 1DS**
Castleton Visitor Centre	**S33 8WN**
Moorland Centre, The,	
Edale Visitor Centre	**S33 7ZA**
Upper Derwent Visitor Centre	**S33 0AQ**
Pembrokeshire National Park	
Newport	**SA42 0TN**
St. Davids	**SA62 6NW**
Tenby	**SA70 7DL**
Queen Elizabeth Forest Park	
David Marshall Lodge	**FK8 3SX**
Sherwood Pines Forest Park	
Sherwood Pines Forest Park	
Visitor Centre	**NG21 9JL**
Snowdonia National Park	
Aberdyfi	**LL35 0EE**
Begggelert	**LL55 4YD**
Betws y Coed	**LL24 0AH**
Blaenau Ffestiniog	**LL41 3ES**
Dolgellau	**LL40 1PU**
Harlech	**LL46 2YE**

Tay Forest Park	
Queen's View Visitor Centre	**PH16 5NR**
The Broads National Park	
Beccles	**NR34 9BH**
Hoveton	**NR12 8UR**
Potter Heigham	**NR29 5JD**
Ranworth	**NR13 6HY**
Whitlington	**NR14 8TR**
Thetford Forest Park	
High Lodge Forest Centre	**IP27 0TJ**
Whinlatter Forest Park	
Visitor Centre	**CA12 5TW**
Yorkshire Dales National Park	
Aysgarth	**DL8 3TH**
Grassington	**BD23 5LB**
Hawes	**DL8 3NT**
Malham	**BD23 4DA**
Reeth	**DL11 6SY**

Out of town shopping centres

Ashford Designer Outlet	**TN24 0SD**
Atlantic Village, Bideford	**EX39 3QU**
Bicester Village	**OX26 6WD**
Bluewater, Kent	**DA9 9ST**
Braehead, Glasgow	**G51 4BP**
Brent Cross, London	**NW4 3FP**
Bridgend Designer Outlet	**CF32 9SU**
Cheshire Oaks Designer Outlet,	
Ellesmere Port	**CH65 9JJ**
Clacton Factory Outlet	**CO15 4TL**
Clarks Village, Street	**BA16 0BB**
Cribbs Causeway, Bristol	**BS34 5DG**
Dalton Park, Seaham	**SR7 9HU**
De Bradelei, Belper	**CT17 9BY**
De Bradelei Wharf, Dover	**CT17 9BY**
Dockside Outlet Centre, Chatham	**ME4 3ED**
East Midlands Designer Outlet,	
Mansfield	**DE55 2JW**
Festival Park, Ebbw Vale	**NP23 8FP**
Freeport, Braintree	**CM77 8YH**
Freeport, Fleetwood	**FY7 6AE**
Freeport, Hornsea	**HU18 1UT**

Galleria, The, Hatfield	**AL10 0XR**
Gretna Gateway	**DG16 5GG**
Gunwharf Quays, Portsmouth	**PO1 3AF**
Jackson's Landing, Hartlepool	**TS24 0XZ**
Junction 32, Castleford	**WF10 4SB**
K Village, Kendal	**LA9 4ND**
Lakeside, Doncaster	**DN4 5JH**
Lakeside, Thurrock	**RM20 2ZP**
Lightwater Village, Ripon	**HG4 3HT**
Livingston Designer Outlet	**EH54 6QX**
Lomond Galleries, Alexandria	**G83 0UE**
Lowry Designer Outlet, Salford	**M50 3AH**
Meadowhall, Sheffield	**S9 1EP**
Merry Hill, Brierley Hill	**DY5 1QX**
MetroCentre, Gateshead	**NE11 9YG**
Royal Quays, Newcastle upon Tyne	**NE29 6DW**
Sterling Mills, Tillicoultry	**FK13 6HQ**
Swindon Designer Outlet	**SN2 2DY**
Trafford Centre, Manchester	**M17 8AA**
Westfield London	**W12 7SL**
York Designer Outlet	**YO19 4TA**

Aberdeen

Dundee

Perth

M90

Stirling

M80 M9

Glasgow

M8 M8 Edinburgh

M77

M74

Dumfries

A74(M)

Stranraer

Carlisle

M6

Newcastle upon Tyne

A194(M)

Middlesbrough

A1(M)

Lancaster

M6

Leeds

A1(M)

Blackpool

M55

M65

Kingston upon Hull

M62

Manchester

M66

M62

M18

M180

Liverpool

M58

M61

M60

A1(M)

Chester

M53 M56

Sheffield

M1

Stoke-on-Trent

Nottingham

M6

Norwich

Aberystwyth

M6 Toll

M42

Leicester

Peterborough

M54

M69

Birmingham

M42

A1(M)

Coventry

Cambridge

M5

M11

M40

Ross-on-Wye

M50

Gloucester

Oxford

A1(M)

Ipswich

Swindon

M1

Swansea

M4

M4

Reading

M4

London

M25

Cardiff

M48

Bristol

M3

M25

M29

M20

M23

Folkestone

M5

Southampton

M27

A3(M)

Brighton

Exeter

Poole

Portsmouth

Plymouth

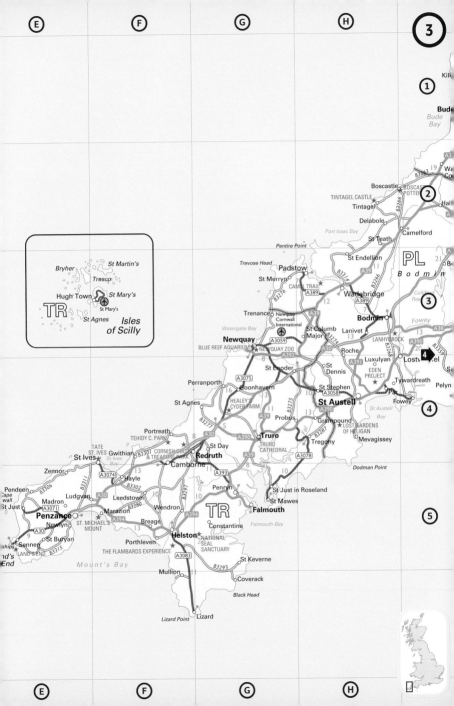

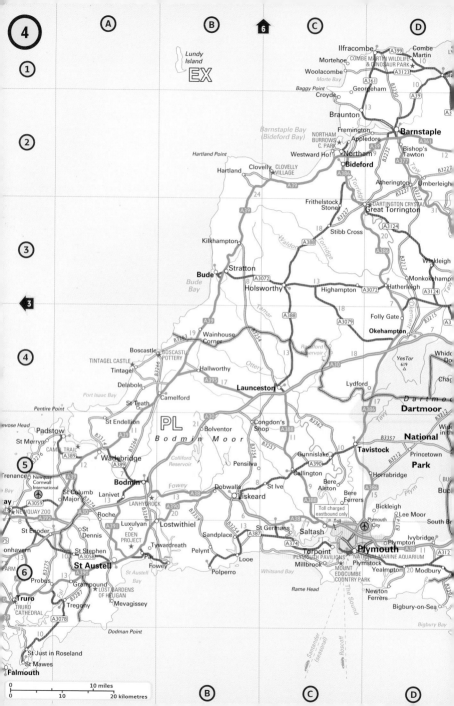

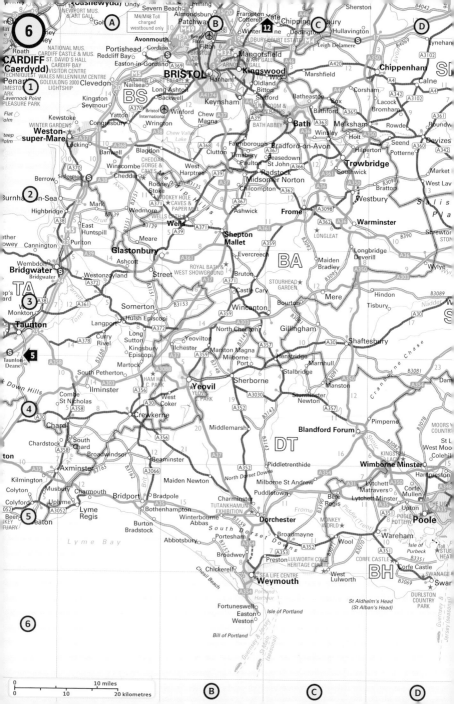

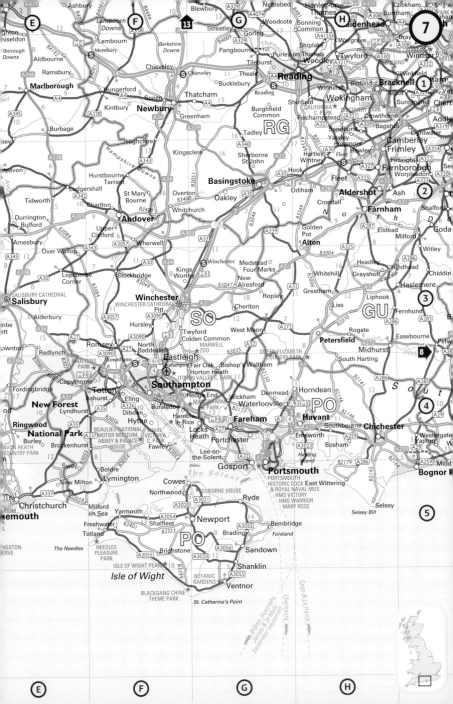

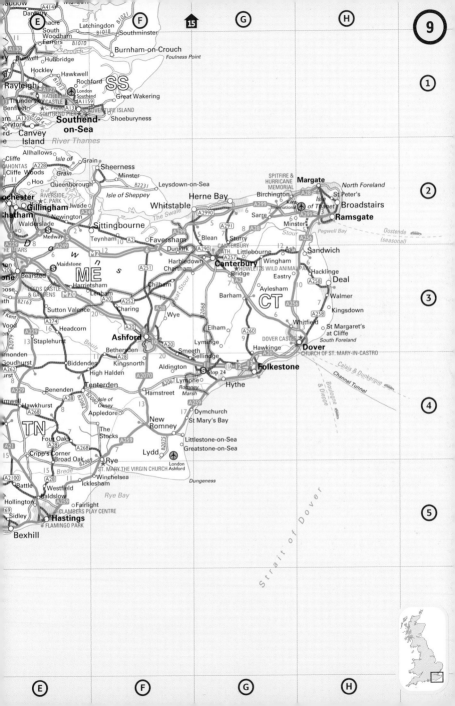

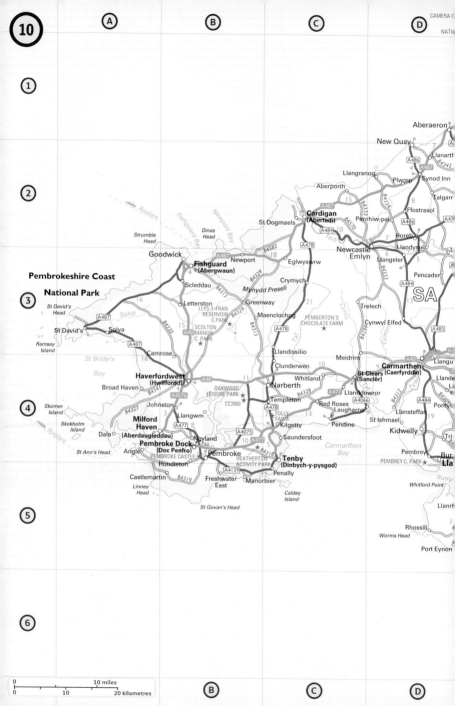

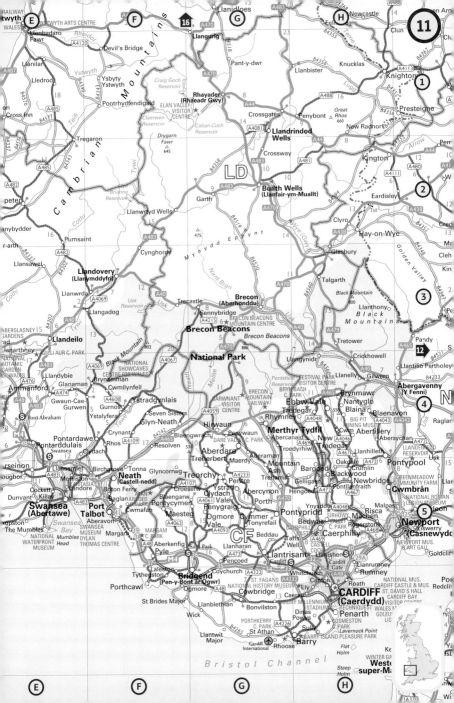

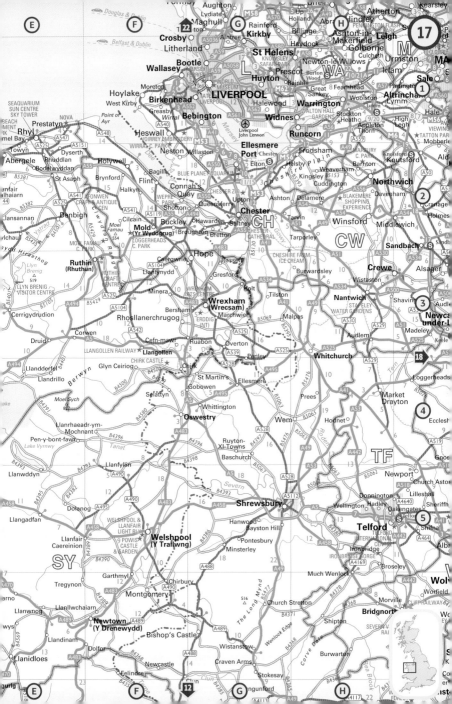

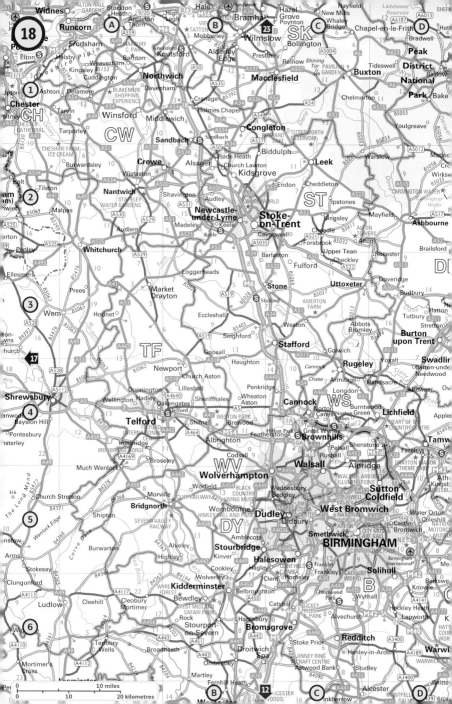

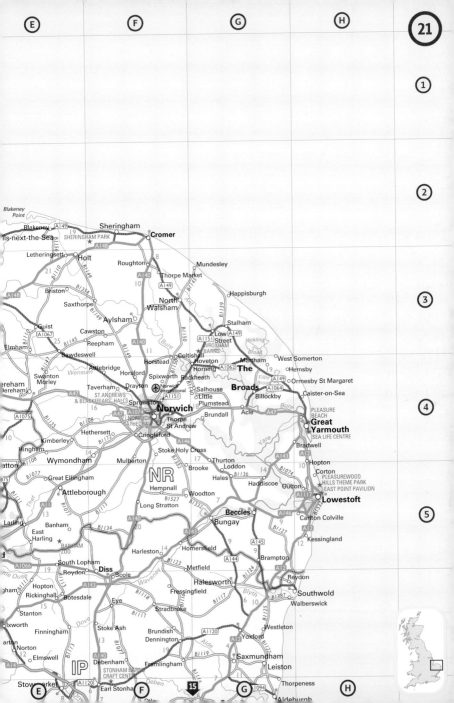

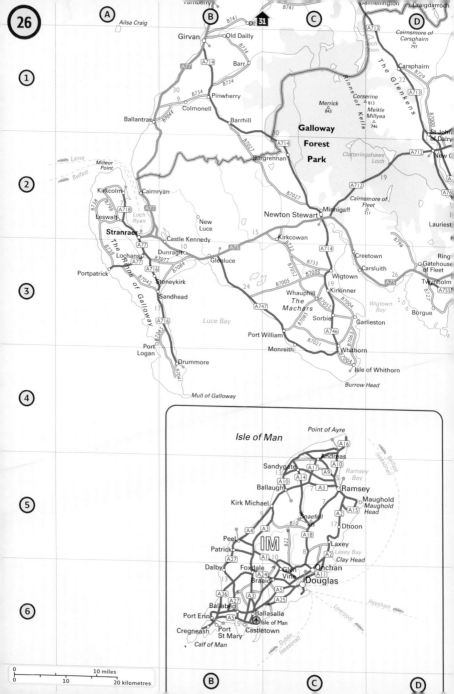

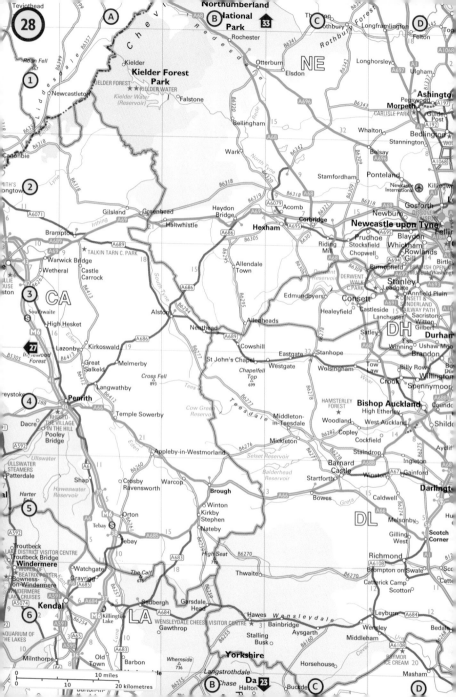

1

2

3

4

5

island

outh

wbiggin-by-the-Sea

yth

ton
Seaton Sluice
ton Delaval
Whitley Bay
BLUE REEF AQUARIUM
nmoor
Tynemouth
North Shields
en
nd
South Shields
Jarrow
SOUTH SHIELDS
MUSEUM & ART
GALLERY
burn
A183
d
Cleadon
Boldon
A1018

Amsterdam
Amsterdam (Toll)

Sunderland
ashington
MUSEUM & WINTER GARDENS
A183
A19
er-le-Street
A1018
SR
nmoor
Hetton
le-Hole
Seaham
10
Muton
South Hetton
Haswell
Easington Colliery
A182
Easington
urn
Peterlee
Horden
mley
Wheatley
Hill
Blackhall Colliery
A181
Wingate
A1086

Trimdon
12
A179
Hartlepool
Fishburn
A19
6
Tees
Bay
ARDWICK HALL
PARK
Sedgefield
A689
A178
A177
8

n
Redcar
Billingham
A1085
South
Bank
Marske-by-the-Sea
Saltburn-by-the-Sea
Middlesbrough
PARK
Eston
Brotton
kton-on-Tees
PARK
Thornaby-on-Tees
B1269
Skelton
Loftus
Eaglescliffe
A171
Guisborough
Hinderwell
A67
Roseberry
Topping
6
16
ham Tees
Valley
Egglescliffe
A174
Sandsend
Yarm
A1273
Great Ayton
Whitby
ST MARY'S
TS
Hutton
Rudby
Danby
Sleights
High
Hawsker
13
Stokesley
A19
Castleton
B1416
8
Great
Broughton
Egton
A172
Robin
Hood's Bay
15
A167
Round Hill
454
Staindale
Brompton
A684
Cleveland
Hills
North York Moors
20
20
ton
Rosedale Abbey
A171
Staintondale
A169
Cloughton
Burniston
North York Moors
NORTH RIDING
FOREST PARK
A165
SEA LIFE &
MARINE SANCTUARY
National Park
Gillamoor
Lockton
Hackness
ng
Knayton
A168
Kirkbymoorside
NORTH YORKSHIRE
MOORS RAILWAY
**North Riding
Forest Park**
Scalby
A167
7
Boltby
A170
Wrelton
DALBY FOREST DRIVE
Scarborough
Thirsk
Helmsley
13
Pickering
17
A170
Seamer
Eastfield
A61
Sproxton
Vale of Pickering
Thornton le-
Dale
Snainton
Cayton
A168
Sowerby
13
Wass
Rye
FLAMINGO
LAND
Derwent
Filey
E
opcliffe
Coxwold
Oswaldkirk
F
24
Hovingham
YO
G
A54
16
H
Staxton
Hunmanby
A1039

Seven

Riccal

Dove

Hambleton
Hills

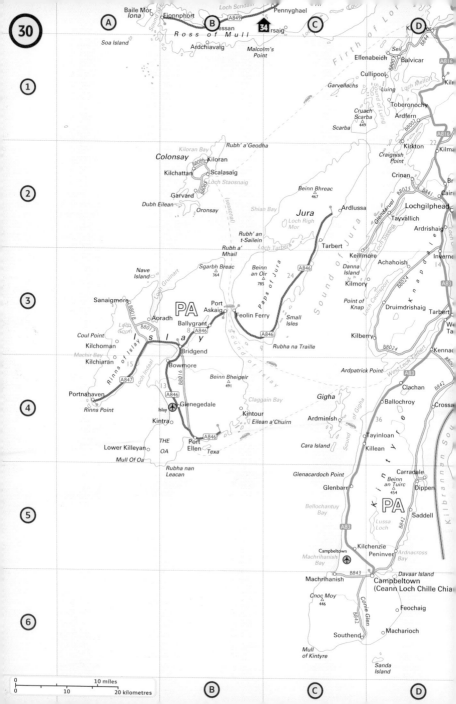

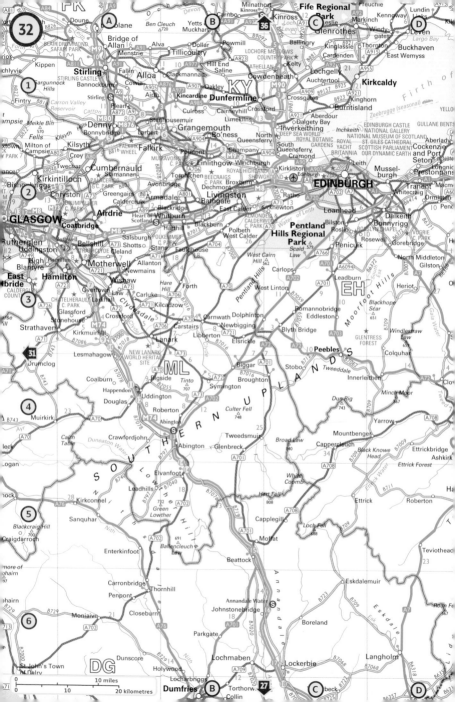

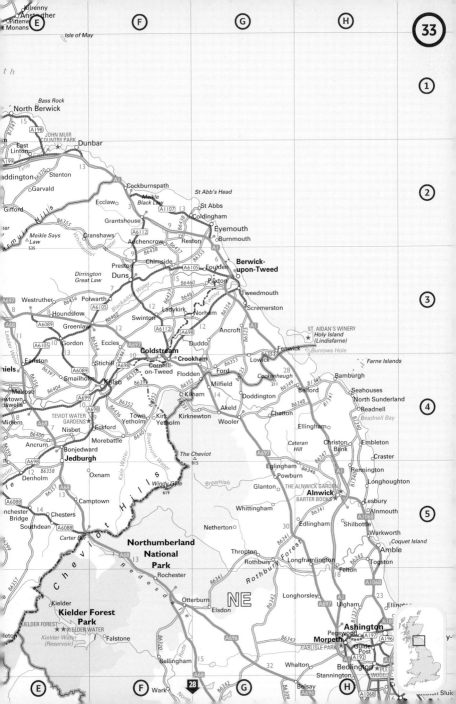

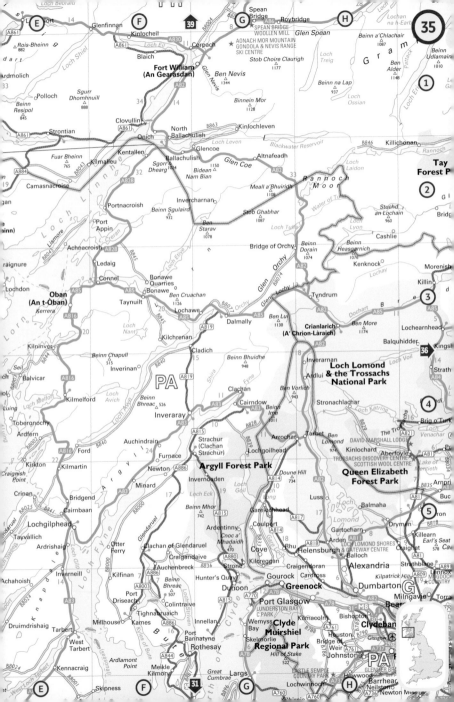

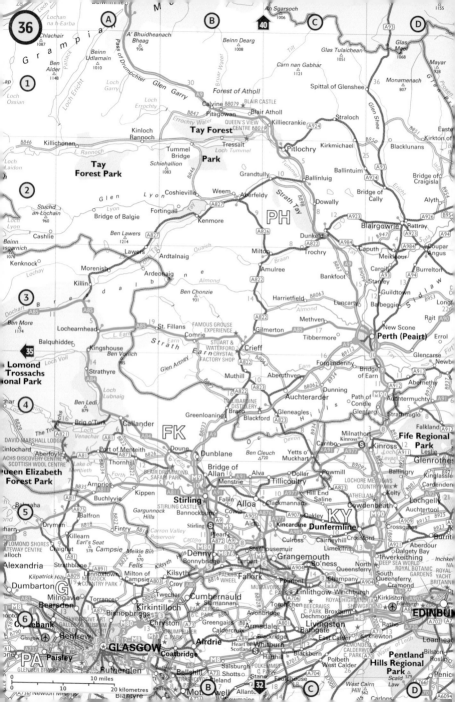

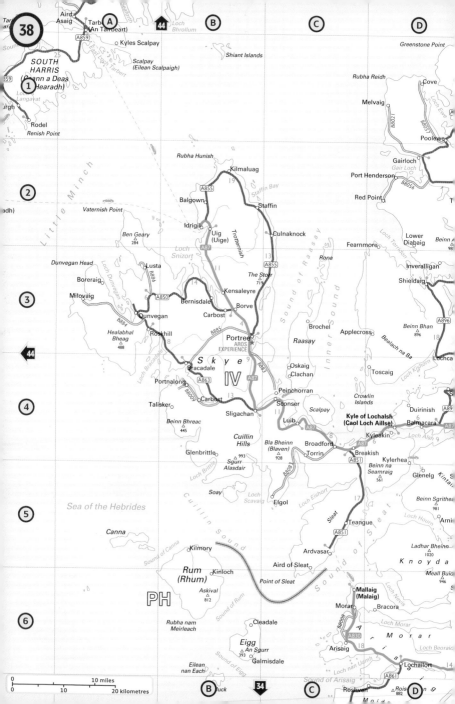

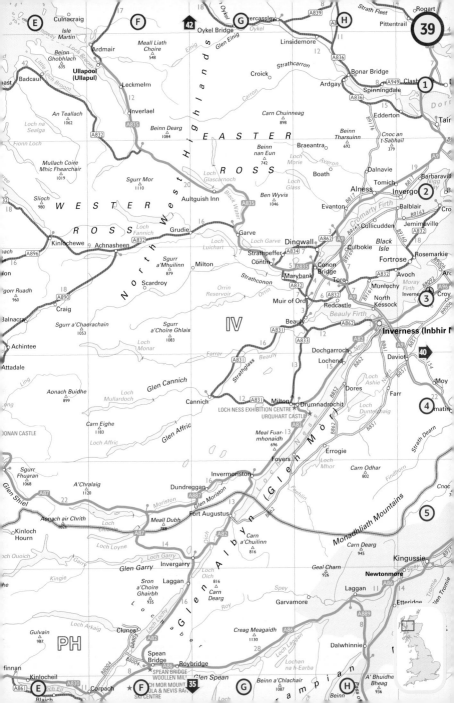

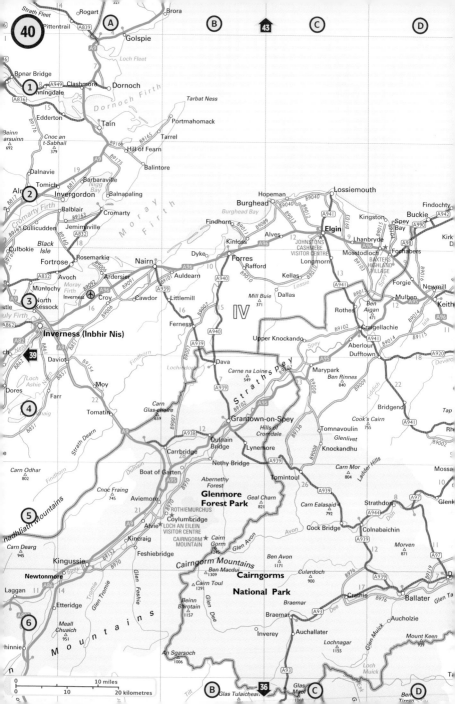

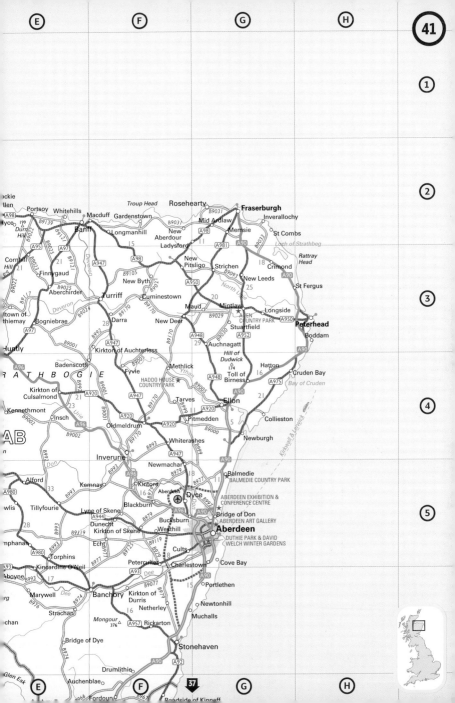

ockie
llen
Portsoy Whitehills
(A98)
yce 199 B9139 Macduff Gardenstown
Durn Banff Longmanhill
Hill B9121 New
B9025 Aberdour
A95 B9023 A97 A98 Ladysford
Cornhill B9023 21
Hill 21 Finnygaud B9105
Aberchirder B9024 New Byth
B9117 Turriff B9170 Cuminestown
Deveron B9024 Darra
own of 28 New Deer
thiemay B9001
Huntly B9024 B992 Kirkton of Auchterless
A97 B9001 A947
STRATHBOGIE Badenscoth B9005 Methlick
Kirkton of Fyvie HADDO HOUSE
Culsalmond A920 B8001 COUNTRY PARK
Kennethmont 23 Ythan A920 Tarves
Insch A96 B9002 Oldmeldrum B9170
AB B993 Whiterashes
Inverurie A947
Alford 33 B993 Newmachar
A980 Kemnay B979 18 B977
wlis B993 Kintore Aberdeen Dyce
Tillyfourie Lyne of Skene A96 Bucksburn
28 B9119 Dunecht Kirkton of Skene Westhill
mphanan Echt B9119 Aberdeen
A980 Torphins B9077 Cults
93 Kincardine O'Neil B977 Peterculter Charlestown
Aboyne B993 17 A93 Dee
rg Marywell Banchory Kirkton of
Strachan B974 Durris Netherley
chan Mongour A957 Rickarton
376 Muchalls
Bridge of Dye
Stonehaven
Glen Esk Drumlithie
Auchenblae Fordoun

Troup Head Rosehearty
Fraserburgh
B9031 Inverallochy
Mid Ardlaw
New Memsie St Combs
Aberdour A98 A90 B9033 Loch of Strathbeg
15 New A981 Rattray
Pitsligo Strichen 18 Crimond Head
A950 B9093 New Leeds A90
North of 25 St Fergus
Maud Mintlaw Longside
A952 A950 Peterhead
Stuartfield Boddam
B9029 ABERDEEN
COUNTRY PARK A90
29 Auchnagatt
Hill of Hatton 16 Cruden Bay
Dudwick A975 Bay of Cruden
174 Toll of
Birness Ellon 21
A948 Colliston
5 A90
Newburgh
Kirriel & Lewis
A90
11 Balmedie
BALMEDIE COUNTRY PARK
ABERDEEN EXHIBITION &
CONFERENCE CENTRE
Bridge of Don
ABERDEEN ART GALLERY
Aberdeen
DUTHIE PARK & DAVID
WELCH WINTER GARDENS
Cove Bay
15 Portlethen
16 Newtonhill

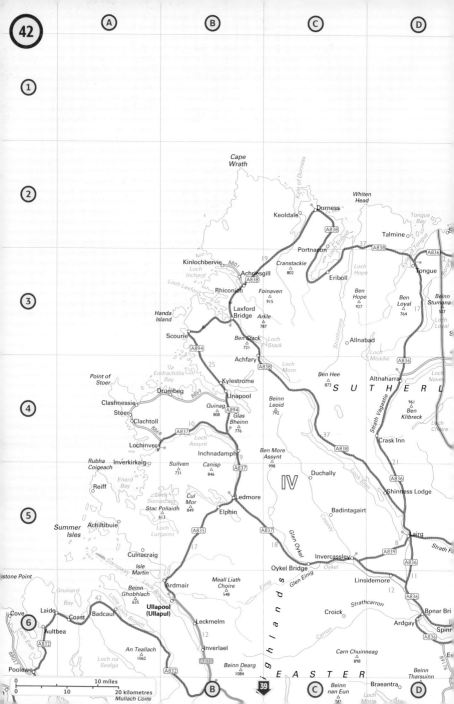

A   B   C   D

1

Cape
Wrath

Whiten
Head

2

Keoldale
Durness

Tongue
Bay

Portnancon
A838
37
A838
Talmine
A836

Cranstackie
802
Loch
Hope
Tongue

Kinlochbervie
B801
19
Eriboll

Achriesgill
A838
Ben
Hope
△ 927
Ben
Loyal
△ 764
Beinn
Stumanadh
△ 527

Rhiconich
Foinaven
△ 915
Loch
Laxford

3

Handa
Island
Laxford
Bridge
Arkle
△ 787
Strathmore

Scourie
Ben Stack
721
Loch
Stack
Allnabad
Loch
Meadie
A836

A894
Achfary
A838
Loch
More
Ben Hee
△ 873
S U T H E R L

Point of
Stoer
Drumbeg
B869
Kylestrome
Unapool

4

Clashnessie
Stoer
Clachtoll
B869
Quinag
△ 808
A894
Glas
Bheinn
△ 776
Beinn
Leoid
△ 792
Strath Vagastie
△ 961
Ben
Klibreck
Altnaharra
Loch
Choirie

Lochinver
A837
Loch
Assynt
Inchnadamph
A837
37
A838
Crask Inn

Rubha
Coigeach
Inverkirkaig
Sullven
△ 731
Canisp
△ 846
Ben More
Assynt
△ 998
Duchally
21
A836

Reiff
Enard
Bay
Loch
Sionascaig
Cul
Mor
△ 849
IV
Shinness Lodge

5

Summer
Isles
Achiltibuie
Stac Pollaidh
△ 613
Loch
Lurgainn
Ledmore
Elphin
A815
A837
Glen Oykel
Cassley
Badintagairt
Lairg
8
A839
Strath F

17
18
Invercassley
A836

stone Point
Isle
Martin
Stramoway Loch
Ardmair
Meall Liath
Choire
△ 548
Oykel Bridge
Oykel
Glen Einig
Linsidemore
11
A836

Gruinard
Bay
Beinn
Ghobhlach
△ 635
Ullapool
(Ullapul)
A835
Einig
Glen Einig
Strathcarron
Croick
12
Bonar Bri

Cove
Laide
Coast
Badcaul
Leckmelm
A835
Carron
Carn Chuinneag
△ 898
Ardgay
A836
Spinn

6

Aultbea
Inverlael
B9176

Poolewe
B8057
An Teallach
△ 1062
Loch na
Sealga
A832
Beinn Dearg
△ 1084
E A S T E R
Braeantra
Beinn
Tharsuinn

0   10 miles
0   10   20 kilometres
Mullach Coire
B
39
C
Beinn
nan Eun
△ 743
Loch
Morie
D

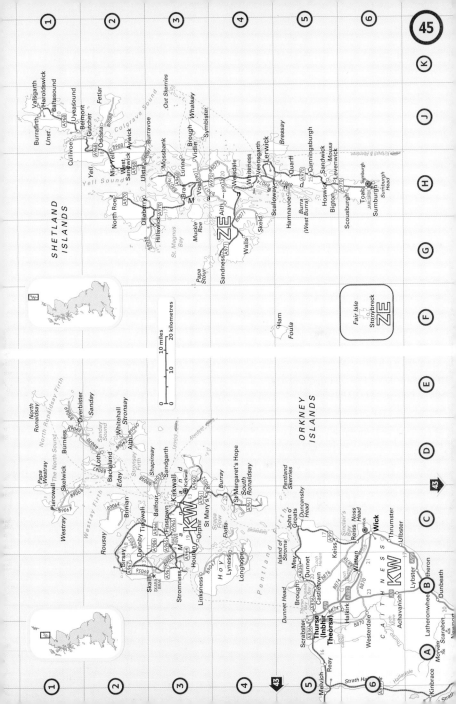

Abbreviations

A&B	Argyll & Bute	ESuss	East Sussex	NELincs	North East	Stir	Stirling
Aber	Aberdeenshire	Edin	Edinburgh		Lincolnshire	Stock	Stockton-on-Tees
B&H	Brighton & Hove	Falk	Falkirk	NLan	North Lanarkshire	Stoke	Stoke-on-Trent
B&NESom	Bath & North East	Flints	Flintshire	NLincs	North Lincolnshire	Suff	Suffolk
	Somerset	Glas	Glasgow	NPT	Neath Port Talbot	Surr	Surrey
B'burn	Blackburn with	Glos	Gloucestershire	NSom	North Somerset	Swan	Swansea
	Darwen	GtLon	Greater London	NYorks	North Yorkshire	T&W	Tyne & Wear
B'pool	Blackpool	GtMan	Greater Manchester	Norf	Norfolk	Tel&W	Telford & Wrekin
BGwent	Blaenau Gwent	Gwyn	Gwynedd	Nott	Nottingham	VGlam	Vale of Glamorgan
Bed	Bedford	Hants	Hampshire	Notts	Nottinghamshire	W&M	Windsor &
Bourne	Bournemouth	Hart	Hartlepool	Ork	Orkney		Maidenhead
BrackF	Bracknell Forest	Here	Herefordshire	Oxon	Oxfordshire	W'ham	Wokingham
Bucks	Buckinghamshire	Herts	Hertfordshire	P&K	Perth & Kinross	WBerks	West Berkshire
Caerp	Caerphilly	High	Highland	Pembs	Pembrokeshire	WDun	West
Cambs	Cambridgeshire	Hull	Kingston upon Hull	Peter	Peterborough		Dunbartonshire
Carmar	Carmarthenshire	Invcly	Inverclyde	Plym	Plymouth	WIsles	Western Isles (Na h-
CenBeds	Central Bedfordshire	IoA	Isle of Anglesey	Ports	Portsmouth		Eileanan an Iar)
Cere	Ceredigion	IoM	Isle of Man	R&C	Redcar & Cleveland	WLoth	West Lothian
ChesE	Cheshire East	IoW	Isle of Wight	RCT	Rhondda Cynon Taff	WMid	West Midlands
ChesW&C	Cheshire West &	Lancs	Lancashire	Renf	Renfrewshire	WSuss	West Sussex
	Chester	Leic	Leicester	Rut	Rutland	WYorks	West Yorkshire
Corn	Cornwall	Leics	Leicestershire	S'end	Southend-on-Sea	Warks	Warwickshire
Cumb	Cumbria	Lincs	Lincolnshire	SAyr	South Ayrshire	Warr	Warrington
D&G	Dumfries &	MK	Milton Keynes	SGlos	South	Wilts	Wiltshire
	Galloway	MTyd	Merthyr Tydfil		Gloucestershire	Worcs	Worcestershire
Denb	Denbighshire	Med	Medway	SLan	South Lanarkshire	Wrex	Wrexham
Derbys	Derbyshire	Mersey	Merseyside	SYorks	South Yorkshire		
Dur	Durham	Middl	Middlesbrough	ScBord	Scottish Borders		
EAyr	East Ayrshire	Midlo	Midlothian	Shet	Shetland		
ELoth	East Lothian	Mon	Monmouthshire	Shrop	Shropshire		
ERid	East Riding of	N'hants	Northamptonshire	Som	Somerset		
	Yorkshire	N'umb	Northumberland	Staffs	Staffordshire		

A

Abbeytown **27** G3
Abbots Bromley **18** C3
Abbotsbury **6** B5
Aberaeron **10** D1
Aberaman **11** G4
Abercanaid **11** G4
Aberchirder **41** E3
Abercynon **11** G5
Aberdare **11** G4
Aberdaron **16** A4
Aberdeen **41** G5
Aberdour **32** C1
Aberdyfi **16** C6
Aberfeldy **36** B2
Aberffraw **16** B2
Aberfoyle **31** H1
Abergavenny
(Y Fenni) **12** A4
Abergele **22** A6
Abergwynolwyn **16** C5
Aberkenfig **11** F5
Aberlady **32** D1
Aberlemno **37** F2
Aberlour **40** C3
Abernethy **36** D4
Aberporth **10** C2
Abersoch **16** B4
Abersychan **11** H4
Abertillery **11** H4
Aberuthven **36** C4
Aberystwyth **16** C6
Abhainnsuidhe **44** C4
Abingdon **13** F5
Abington **32** B4
Aboyne **41** E6
Abram **22** D4
Accrington **23** E3
Achadh Mòr **44** E3
Achahoish **30** D3
Acharacle **34** D1
Achavanich **43** G3
Achfary **42** B3
Achiltibuie **42** A5

Achintee **39** E3
Achnacroish **35** E2
Achnasheen **39** F3
Achosnich **34** C1
Achriesgill **42** B3
Ackworth Moor
Top **24** B4
Acle **21** G4
Acomb **28** C2
Adderbury **13** F3
Addingham **23** F2
Addlestone **14** A6
Adlington **22** D4
Adwick le Street **24** C4
Ainsdale **22** C4
Aintree **22** C5
Aird Asaig **44** D4
Aird of Sleat **38** C5
Airdrie **32** A2
Airidh a'Bhruaich **44** D4
Airth **32** A1
Airton **23** E2
Aith *Ork* **45** C7
Aith *Shet* **45** H4
Akeld **33** G4
Albrighton **18** B4
Alcester **12** D2
Aldbourne **13** E6
Aldbrough **25** F3
Aldeburgh **15** H2
Aldenham **14** B5
Alderbury **7** E3
Alderholt **7** E4
Alderley Edge **23** E6
Aldershot **7** H2
Aldingham **22** B1
Aldington **9** F4
Aldridge **18** C4
Alexandria **31** G3
Alford *Aber* **41** E5
Alford *Lincs* **25** G6
Alfreton **19** E2
Allanton **32** A3
Allendale Town **28** B3
Allenheads **28** B3
Allhallows **15** E6

Allnabad **42** C3
Alloa **32** A1
Allonby **27** F3
Alloway **31** G6
Almondsbury **12** B5
Alness **39** H2
Alnmouth **33** H5
Alnwick **33** H5
Alresford **15** F3
Alrewas **18** D4
Alsager **18** B2
Alston **28** B3
Altnafeadh **35** G2
Altnaharra **42** D4
Alton *Hants* **7** H3
Alton *Staffs* **18** D2
Altrincham **23** E5
Alva **32** A1
Alvechurch **12** D1
Alveley **18** B5
Alveston **12** B5
Alvie **40** A5
Alyth **36** D2
Ambergate **19** E2
Amble **33** H5
Amblecote **18** B5
Ambleside **27** H5
Ambrosden **13** G4
Amersham **14** A5
Amesbury **7** E2
Amlwch **16** B1
Ammanford **11** E4
Ampthill **14** A3
Amulree **36** B3
Ancaster **19** H2
Ancroft **33** G3
Ancrum **32** D4
Andover **7** F2
Andreas **26** C5
Angle **10** A4
Angmering **8** A5
Anlaby **25** F5
Annan **27** G2
Annbank **31** G5
Annfield Plain **28** D3

Anstey **19** F4
Anstruther **37** F4
Aoradh **30** A3
Appleby Magna **19** E4
Appleby-in-
Westmorland **28** A4
Applecross **38** D3
Appledore *Devon* **4** C2
Appledore *Kent* **9** F4
Appleton Thorn **22** D5
Appley Bridge **22** D4
Arbirlot **37** F2
Arbroath **37** F2
Archiavaig **30** B1
Arden **31** G2
Ardentinny **31** F2
Ardeonaig **36** A3
Ardersier **40** A3
Ardfern **30** D1
Ardgay **39** H1
Ardleigh **15** F3
Ardlui **31** G1
Ardlussa **30** C2
Ardmair **39** F1
Ardminish **30** C4
Ardmolich **35** E1
Ardnahaig **30** D2
Ardrossan **31** F4
Ardtalnaig **36** A3
Ardtoe **34** D1
Ardvasar **38** C5
Annagour **34** B2
Arisaig **38** C6
Armadale **32** B2
Armitage **18** C4
Armthorpe **24** C4
Arncliffe **23** F1
Arnisdale **38** D5
Arnol **44** E2
Arnold **19** F2
Arnprior **31** H2
Arrochar **31** G1
Arundel **8** A5
Ascot **14** A6
Asfordby **19** G4
Ash *Kent* **9** G3

Ash *Surr* **7** H2
Ashbourne **18** D2
Ashburton **5** E5
Ashbury **13** E5
Ashby de la Zouch **19** E4
Ashchurch **12** D3
Ashcott **6** A3
Ashford *Kent* **9** F3
Ashford *Surr* **14** A6
Ashington **28** D1
Ashkirk **32** D4
Ashley **14** D1
Ashton **24** D6
Ashton-in-
Makerfield **22** D5
Ashton-under-
Lyne **23** F5
Ashurst *Hants* **7** F4
Ashurst *Kent* **8** D4
Ashwick **6** B2
Askern **24** C4
Aspatria **27** G3
Aston Clinton **13** H4
Aston on Trent **19** E3
Astwood Bank **12** D1
Atherington **4** D2
Atherstone **19** E5
Atherton **22** D4
Attadale **39** E4
Attleborough **21** E5
Attlebridge **21** F4
Auchallater **40** C6
Auchenblae **37** G1
Auchenbreck **31** E2
Auchencairn **27** E3
Auchencrow **33** F2
Auchindrain **31** E1
Auchinleck **31** H5
Auchmull **37** F1
Auchnagatt **41** G3
Aucholzie **40** D6
Auchterarder **36** C4
Auchtermuchty **36** D4
Auchtertool **32** C1
Audlem **18** A2
Audley **18** B2

Aughton *Lancs* 22 C4
Aughton *SYorks* 24 B5
Auldearn 40 B3
Aultbea 38 D1
Aultguish Inn 39 G2
Aveley 14 D5
Aviemore 40 A5
Avoch 39 H3
Avonbridge 32 B2
Avonmouth 12 B6
Awre 12 C4
Awsworth 19 E2
Axminster 5 G4
Aycliffe 28 D4
Aylesbury 13 H4
Aylesford 9 E3
Aylesham 9 G3
Aylsham 21 F3
Ayr 31 G5
Aysgarth 28 C6
Aywick 45 J2

B

Babworth 24 C5
Backaland 45 D2
Backwell 12 A6
Bacup 23 E3
Badcaul 39 E1
Badenscoth 41 E4
Badintagairt 42 C5
Badlipster 43 G3
Badsey 12 D2
Bagillt 22 B6
Baglan 11 F5
Bagshot 14 A6
Baildon 24 A3
Baile Mhartainn 44 B6
Baile Mòr 34 B3
Bainbridge 28 C6
Bainton 25 E2
Bakewell 24 A6
Bala (Y Bala) 17 E4
Balallan 44 D3
Balbeggie 36 D3
Balblair 40 A2
Balcombe 8 C4
Balderton 19 G2
Baldock 14 B3
Baldslow 9 E5
Balemartine 34 A2
Balephuil 34 A2
Balfour 45 C3
Balfron 31 H2
Balgown 38 B2
Balintore 40 A2
Balivanich 44 B7
Ballabeg 26 B6
Ballachulish 35 F2
Ballantrae 26 A1
Ballasalla 26 B6
Ballater 40 D6
Ballaugh 26 C5
Ballingry 32 C1
Ballinluig 36 C2
Ballintuim 36 D2
Balloch 31 G2
Ballochroy 30 D4
Ballygrant 30 B3
Balmacara 38 D4
Balmaha 31 G2
Balmedie 41 G5
Balnacra 39 E3
Balnahard 34 C3
Balnapaling 40 A2
Balquhidder 36 A3
Baltasound 45 J1
Balvicar 30 D1
Bamburgh 33 H4
Bampton *Devon* 5 F2
Bampton *Oxon* 13 F4
Banbury 13 F2

Banchory 41 F6
Banff 41 E2
Bangor 16 C1
Banham 21 E5
Bankfoot 36 C3
Bannockburn 32 A1
Banstead 8 B3
Banwell 6 A2
Bar Hill 14 C1
Barassie 31 G5
Barbon 28 A6
Barby 13 G1
Bardney 25 F6
Bardsea 22 C1
Bargoed 11 H5
Bargrennan 26 C2
Barham 9 G3
Barking 14 C5
Barkston 19 H2
Barkway 14 C3
Barlaston 18 B3
Barlborough 24 B6
Barley 14 C3
Barmouth 16 C5
Barnard Castle 28 C5
Barnet 14 B4
Barningham 15 F1
Barnoldswick 23 E2
Barnsley 24 B4
Barnstaple 4 D2
Barnton 22 D6
Barr 26 B1
Barrapoll 34 A2
Barrhead 31 H4
Barrhill 26 B1
Barrock 43 G2
Barrow upon
  Humber 25 E3
Barrow upon Soar 19 F4
Barrowford 23 E2
Barrow-in-Furness 22 B1
Barry 11 H6
Barton 22 D3
Barton-le-Clay 14 A3
Barton-under-
  Needwood 18 D4
Barton-upon-
  Humber 25 E3
Barvas 44 E2
Baschurch 17 G4
Basildon 15 E5
Basingstoke 7 G2
Baslow 24 A6
Bassingham 25 E6
Bath 12 C6
Batheaston 12 C6
Bathford 12 C6
Bathgate 32 B2
Batley 24 A3
Battle 9 E5
Bawdeswell 21 E3
Bawdsey 15 H2
Bawtry 24 C5
Baycliff 22 B1
Bayston Hill 17 G5
Beaconsfield 14 A5
Beadnell 33 H4
Beaminster 6 A4
Bearsden 31 H3
Bearsted 9 E3
Beattock 32 B5
Beauly 39 H3
Beaumaris 16 C2
Beccles 21 G5
Beckingham 24 D5
Bedale 28 D6
Beddau 11 G5
Beddgelert 16 C3
Beddingham 8 C5
Bedford 14 A2
Bedlington 28 D1

Bedwas 11 H5
Bedworth 19 E5
Beeford 25 F2
Beer 5 G4
Beeston 19 F3
Beighton 24 B5
Beith 31 G4
Belbroughton 12 D1
Belford 33 H4
Bellingham 28 B1
Bellshill 32 A3
Belmont 45 J1
Belper 19 E2
Belsay 28 D2
Bembridge 7 G5
Bempton 25 F1
Benenden 9 E4
Benllech 16 C1
Benson 13 G5
Bentley 24 C4
Bere Alston 4 C5
Bere Ferrers 4 C5
Bere Regis 6 C5
Berinsfield 13 G5
Berkeley 12 B5
Berkhamsted 14 A4
Berkswell 13 E1
Bernisdale 38 B3
Berriedale 43 G4
Berrow 5 G1
Bersham 17 G3
Berwick-upon-
  Tweed 33 G3
Bessacarr 24 C4
Bethersden 9 F3
Bethesda 16 C2
Bettyhill 43 E2
Betws-y-coed 16 D3
Beverley 25 E3
Bewdley 12 C1
Bexhill 9 E5
Bexley 14 C6
Bexleyheath 14 C6
Bibury 13 E4
Bicester 13 G3
Bickleigh (Plymouth)
  Devon 4 D5
Bickleigh (Tiverton)
  Devon 5 F3
Bicknacre 15 E4
Biddenden 9 E4
Biddulph 18 B2
Bideford 4 C2
Bidford-on-Avon 12 D2
Bigbury-on-Sea 4 D6
Biggar 32 B4
Biggin Hill 8 C3
Biggleswade 14 B2
Bigton 45 H5
Bilbster 43 G3
Billericay 14 D5
Billinge 22 D4
Billingham 29 E4
Billinghay 20 A2
Billingshurst 8 A4
Billockby 21 G4
Billy Row 28 D4
Bilston 32 C2
Bilton 25 F3
Binbrook 25 F5
Binfield 13 H6
Bingham 19 G3
Bingley 23 A3
Birchgrove 11 F5
Birchington 15 G6
Bircotes 24 C5
Birkenhead 22 C5
Birmingham 18 C5
Birsay 45 B2
Birstall 19 F4
Birtley 28 D3
Bishop Auckland 28 D4
Bishopbriggs 31 H3

Bishop's Castle 17 G6
Bishop's Cleeve 12 D3
Bishop's Hull 5 G2
Bishop's
  Itchington 13 F2
Bishop's Lydeard 5 G2
Bishop's Stortford 14 C3
Bishop's Tawton 4 D2
Bishop's Waltham 7 G4
Bishopston 11 E5
Bishopton 31 G3
Bisley 12 D4
Bitton 12 B6
Blaby 19 F5
Black Bourton 13 E4
Black Notley 15 E3
Blackburn *Aber* 41 F5
Blackburn *B'burn* 22 D3
Blackburn *WLoth* 32 B2
Blackford 36 B4
Blackhall Colliery 29 E4
Blacklunans 36 D1
Blackmoor Gate 4 D1
Blackpool 22 B3
Blackridge 32 A2
Blackwaterfoot 31 E5
Blackwood 11 H5
Blaenau
  Ffestiniog 16 C3
Blaenavon 11 H4
Blaengarw 11 H5
Blaengwrach 11 F4
Blagdon 6 A2
Blaich 35 F1
Blaina 11 H4
Blair Atholl 36 B1
Blairgowrie 36 D2
Blakeney *Glos* 12 B4
Blakeney *Norf* 21 E2
Blandford Forum 6 C4
Blaydon 28 D2
Blean 15 G6
Bletchley 13 H3
Blewbury 13 G5
Blisworth 13 H2
Blockley 13 E3
Bloxham 13 F3
Blubberhouses 24 A2
Blyth *N'umb* 29 E1
Blyth *Notts* 24 C5
Blyth Bridge 32 C3
Blyton 24 D5
Boat of Garten 40 B5
Boath 39 H2
Boddam 41 H3
Bodelwyddan 22 A6
Bodenham 12 B2
Bodicote 13 F2
Bodmin 3 H3
Bogniebrae 41 E3
Bognor Regis 8 A6
Boldon 29 E2
Boldre 7 F5
Bollington 23 F6
Bolnhurst 14 A2
Bolsover 24 B6
Boltby 29 E6
Bolton *ELoth* 33 E2
Bolton *GtMan* 23 E5
Bolton-le-Sands 22 C1
Bolventor 4 B5
Bonar Bridge 39 H1
Bonawe 35 F3
Bonawe Quarries 35 F3
Bonchester Bridge 33 E5
Bo'ness 32 B1
Bonjedward 33 E4
Bonnybridge 32 A1
Bonnyrigg 32 D2
Bonvilston 11 G6
Bootle *Cumb* 27 G6
Bootle *Mersey* 22 C5
Boreham 15 E4

Borehamwood 14 B5
Boreland 27 G1
Boreraig 38 A3
Borgh 44 A9
Borgue *D&G* 26 D3
Borgue *High* 43 G4
Borough Green 8 D3
Boroughbridge 24 B1
Borrowash 19 E3
Borrowdale 27 G2
Borth 16 C6
Borve *High* 38 B3
Borve *Wisles* 44 E2
Bosbury 12 B2
Boscastle 4 B4
Bosham 7 H4
Boston 20 B2
Boston Spa 24 B2
Botesdale 15 F1
Bothel 27 G4
Bothenhampton 6 A5
Bottesford *Leics* 19 G3
Bottesford *NLincs* 25 E4
Boughton 24 C6
Bourne 20 A3
Bourne End 13 H5
Bournemouth 6 D5
Bournmoor 29 E3
Bourton 6 C3
Bourton-on-the-
  Water 13 E3
Bovey Tracey 5 E5
Bowburn 29 E4
Bowes 28 C5
Bowmore 30 B4
Bowness-on-
  Solway 27 G2
Bowness-on-
  Windermere 27 H6
Box 12 C6
Bozeat 14 A2
Braaid 26 C6
Bracadale 38 B4
Bracebridge Heath 25 E6
Brackley 13 G3
Bracknell 13 H6
Braco 36 B4
Bracora 38 D6
Bradford 24 A3
Bradford-on-Avon 12 C6
Brading 7 G5
Bradninch 5 F3
Bradpole 6 A5
Bradshaw 23 E4
Bradwell *Derbys* 24 A5
Bradwell *Norf* 21 H4
Bradwell
  Waterside 15 F4
Brae 45 H3
Braeantra 39 H2
Braemar 40 C6
Bragar 44 D2
Brailsford 18 D2
Braintree 15 E3
Braithwaite 27 G4
Braithwell 24 C5
Bramford 15 G2
Bramhall 23 E5
Bramley 24 B5
Brampton *Cambs* 14 B1
Brampton *Cumb* 28 A2
Brampton *Suff* 21 G5
Brancaster 20 D2
Brandesburton 25 F2
Brandon *Dur* 28 D4
Brandon *Suff* 20 D5
Branston 25 E6
Brantham 15 G3
Bratton 6 D2
Braunston 13 G1
Braunstone 19 F4
Braunton 4 C2
Bray 14 A6

Brayton **24** C3
Breage **3** F5
Breakish **38** C4
Bream **12** B4
Breanais **44** C3
Breascleit **44** D3
Breaston **19** E3
Brechfa **11** E3
Brechin **37** F1
Brecon
  (Aberhonddu) **11** G3
Bredbury **23** F5
Bredon **12** D3
Brentwood **14** D5
Bretton **22** C6
Brewood **18** B4
Bridge **9** G3
Bridge of Allan **32** A1
Bridge of Balgie **36** A2
Bridge of Cally **36** D2
Bridge of Craigisla **36** D2
Bridge of Don **41** G5
Bridge of Dun **37** F2
Bridge of Dye **41** E6
Bridge of Earn **36** D4
Bridge of Orchy **35** H3
Bridge of Weir **31** G3
Bridgend *Angus* **37** F1
Bridgend (Islay)
  A&B **30** B3
Bridgend (Lochgilphead)
  A&B **30** D2
Bridgend (Pen-y-bont ar
  Ogwr) *Bridgend* **11** G6
Bridgend *Moray* **40** D4
Bridgnorth **18** B5
Bridgwater **5** G2
Bridlington **25** F1
Bridport **6** A5
Brierfield **23** E3
Brig o'Turk **31** H1
Brigg **25** E4
Brigham **27** F4
Brighouse **24** A3
Brighstone **7** F5
Brightlingsea **15** F4
Brighton **8** C5
Brigstock **19** H5
Brimington **24** B6
Brinian **45** C2
Brinsley **19** E2
Brinsworth **24** B5
Bristol **12** B6
Briston **21** E3
Briton Ferry **11** F5
Brixham **5** F6
Brixworth **13** H1
Broad Haven **10** A4
Broad Oak **9** E5
Broadclyst **5** H4
Broadford **38** C4
Broadheath **12** B1
Broadmayne **6** C5
Broadstairs **15** H6
Broadway **12** D3
Broadwey **6** B5
Broadwindsor **6** A4
Brochel **38** C3
Brockenhurst **7** F4
Brockworth **12** C4
Brodick **31** E5
Bromham *Bed* **14** A2
Bromham *Wilts* **12** D6
Bromley **14** C6
Brompton **29** E6
Brompton on
  Swale **28** D5
Bromsgrove **12** B2
Bromyard **12** B2
Bronaber **16** D4
Brooke **21** F5
Brookmans Park **14** B4
Broomfield **15** E4

Brora **43** F5
Broseley **18** A4
Brotton **29** F4
Brough *Cumb* **28** B5
Brough *ERid* **25** E3
Brough *High* **43** G2
Brough *Shet* **45** J3
Broughton *Flints* **22** C6
Broughton *NLincs* **25** E4
Broughton
  N'hants **13** H1
Broughton
  ScBord **32** C4
Broughton Astley **19** F5
Broughton in
  Furness **27** G6
Broughty Ferry **37** E3
Brownhills **18** C4
Broxburn **32** B2
Brundall **21** G4
Brundish **15** G1
Bruton **6** B3
Brynamman **11** F4
Brynford **22** B6
Brynmawr **11** H4
Bubwith **24** D3
Buchlyvie **31** H2
Buckden *Cambs* **14** B1
Buckden *NYorks* **23** F1
Buckfastleigh **5** E5
Buckhaven **32** C2
Buckie **40** D2
Buckingham **13** G3
Bucklebury **13** G6
Buckley (Bwcle) **22** B6
Bucksburn **41** F5
Bude **4** B3
Budleigh Salterton **5** F4
Bugbrooke **13** G2
Builth Wells (Llanfair-ym-
  Muallt) **11** G2
Buldoo **43** F3
Bulford **7** E2
Bulkington **19** E5
Bulmer Tye **15** E3
Bunessan **34** C3
Bungay **21** G5
Buntingford **14** C3
Burbage **13** E6
Bures **15** F3
Burford **13** E4
Burgess Hill **8** C5
Burgh by Sands **27** H3
Burgh le Marsh **25** G6
Burghead **40** D2
Burghfield
  Common **13** G6
Burghill **12** A2
Burley **7** E4
Burley in
  Wharfedale **24** A2
Burness **45** D1
Burnham **14** A5
Burnham Market **20** D2
Burnham-on-
  Crouch **15** F5
Burnham-on-Sea **6** A2
Burnhouse **31** G4
Burniston **29** H6
Burnley **23** E3
Burnmouth **33** G2
Burnopfield **28** D3
Burntisland **32** C1
Burntwood Green **18** C4
Burrafirth **45** J1
Burravoe **45** J2
Burrelton **36** D3
Burry Port **10** D4
Burscough **22** C4
Burscough Bridge **22** C4
Bursledon **7** F4
Burton Bradstock **6** A5
Burton Joyce **19** F2

Burton Latimer **14** A1
Burton Leonard **24** B1
Burton upon
  Stather **24** D4
Burton upon
  Trent **18** D3
Burton-in-Kendal **22** D1
Burwardsley **18** A2
Burwarton **18** A5
Burwash **8** D4
Burwell **14** D1
Bury **23** E4
Bury St. Edmunds **15** E1
Bushey **14** B5
Buttercrambe **24** C2
Butterwick **25** E1
Buxted **8** C4
Buxton **23** F6
Byfield **13** G2
Byfleet **14** A6
Bylchau **22** A6

C

Caerau **11** H6
Caergwrle **17** G3
Caerhun **16** D2
Caerleon **12** A5
Caernarfon **16** B2
Caerphilly **11** H5
Caerwent **12** A5
Cairnbaan **30** D2
Cairndow **31** F1
Cairneyhill **32** B1
Cairnryan **26** A2
Caister-on-Sea **21** H4
Caistor **25** E5
Caldbeck **27** H4
Caldecott **19** G5
Caldercruix **32** A2
Caldicot **12** A5
Caldwell **28** D5
Calgary **34** C2
Callander **31** H1
Callington **4** C5
Calne **12** D6
Calver **24** A6
Calverton **19** F2
Calvine **36** B1
Cam **12** C5
Camasnacroise **35** E2
Camberley **13** H6
Camborne **3** F4
Cambourne **14** C2
Cambridge **14** C2
Camden Town **14** B5
Camelford **4** B4
Campbeltown (Ceann
  Chille Chiarain) **30** D6
Camptown **33** E5
Camrose **10** B4
Cannich **39** G4
Cannington **5** G2
Cannock **18** C4
Canonbie **27** H2
Canterbury **9** G3
Canton **11** H6
Canvey Island **15** E5
Caolas **34** A2
Capel **8** B3
Capel Curig **16** D3
Capel St. Mary **15** F3
Cappercleuch **32** C4
Capplegill **32** C5
Caputh **36** C2
Carbost (Loch Snizort
  Beag) *High* **38** B3
Carbost (Loch Harport)
  High **38** B4
Carcroft **24** C4
Cardenden **32** C1
Cardiff (Caerdydd) **11** H6
Cardigan (Aberteifi) **10** C2

Cardross **31** G3
Cargenbridge **27** F2
Cargill **36** D3
Carlisle **27** H3
Carlops **32** C3
Carloway **44** D2
Carlton **19** F2
Carlton Colville **21** H5
Carlton in Lindrick **24** C5
Carlton-on-Trent **24** D6
Carluke **32** A3
Carmarthen
  (Caerfyrddin) **10** D4
Carmyllie **37** F2
Carnbee **37** F4
Carnbo **36** C4
Carnforth **22** C1
Carno **17** E6
Carnoustie **37** F3
Carnwath **32** B3
Carradale **30** D5
Carrbridge **40** B4
Carronbridge **27** E1
Carsaig **34** D3
Carsluith **26** C3
Carsphairn **26** D1
Carstairs **32** B3
Carterton **13** E4
Cartmel **22** C1
Cashlie **35** H2
Castle Bromwich **18** D5
Castle Carrock **28** A3
Castle Cary **6** B3
Castle Donington **19** E3
Castle Douglas **27** E2
Castle Kennedy **26** B3
Castlebay (Bàgh a'
  Chaisteil) **44** A10
Castleford **24** B3
Castlemartin **10** B5
Castleside **28** C3
Castleton **29** F5
Castletown *High* **43** G2
Castletown *IoM* **26** B6
Caterham **8** C3
Caton **22** D1
Catrine **31** H5
Catshill **12** D1
Catterick **28** D6
Catterick Camp **28** D6
Caverswall **18** C2
Cawdor **40** A3
Cawood **24** C3
Cawston **21** F3
Caythorpe **19** H2
Cayton **29** H6
Ceann a' Bhàigh **44** B6
Cearsiadar **44** E3
Cefn-mawr **17** F3
Ceres **37** E4
Cerrigydrudion **17** E3
Chadderton **23** F4
Chagford **5** E4
Chailey **8** C5
Chalfont St. Giles **14** A5
Chalford **12** C4
Chalgrove **13** G5
Champany **32** B2
Chapel
  St. Leonards **25** H6
Chapel-en-le-Frith **23** F5
Chapeltown **24** B5
Chard **6** A4
Chardstock **6** A4
Charfield **12** C5
Charing **9** F3
Charlbury **13** F4
Charlestown **41** G5
Charlesworth **23** F5
Charlton *Hants* **7** F2
Charlton *Wilts* **12** D5
Charlton Kings **12** D3
Charlwood **8** B3

Charminster **6** B5
Charmouth **6** A5
Chartham **9** G3
Chatham **15** E6
Chatteris **20** B5
Chatton **33** G4
Cheadle *GtMan* **23** E5
Cheadle *Staffs* **18** C2
Checkley **18** C3
Chedburgh **15** E2
Cheddar **6** A2
Cheddleton **18** C2
Chelmorton **24** A6
Chelmsford **15** E4
Cheltenham **12** D3
Chepstow
  (Cas-gwent) **12** B5
Cheriton **7** G3
Chertsey **14** A6
Chesham **14** A4
Cheshunt **14** C4
Chester **22** C6
Chesterfield **24** B6
Chester-le-Street **28** D3
Chesters **33** E5
Chew Magna **12** B6
Chichester **7** H4
Chickerell **6** B5
Chiddingfold **8** A4
Chieveley **13** F6
Chigwell **14** C5
Chilcompton **6** B2
Childrey **13** F5
Chilham **9** F3
Chilton **28** D4
Chingford **14** C5
Chinnor **13** H4
Chippenham **12** D6
Chipping Campden **13** E3
Chipping Norton **13** F3
Chipping Ongar **14** D4
Chipping Sodbury **12** C5
Chirbury **17** F6
Chirk **17** F4
Chirnside **33** F3
Chiseldon **13** E5
Chopwell **28** D3
Chorley **22** D4
Chorleywood **14** A5
Christchurch **7** E5
Christon Bank **33** H4
Chryston **31** H3
Chudleigh **5** E3
Chulmleigh **4** D3
Church Aston **18** B4
Church Lawton **18** B2
Church Stretton **17** G6
Churchdown **12** C3
Cilcain **22** B6
Cille Bhrighde **44** B9
Cinderford **12** B4
Cirencester **12** D4
Clabhach **34** B2
Clachan (Loch Fyne)
  A&B **31** F1
Clachan (Kintyre)
  A&B **30** D4
Clachan *High* **38** C4
Clachan of
  Glendaruel **31** E2
Clachtoll **42** A4
Clackmannan **32** B1
Clacton-on-Sea **15** G4
Cladich **35** F3
Claggan **35** E2
Clanfield **13** E4
Claonaig **30** D4
Clapham *Bed* **14** A2
Clapham *NYorks* **23** E1
Clarborough **24** D5
Clare **15** E2
Clashmore **40** A1
Clashnessie **42** A4

Clavering 14 C3
Clay Cross 24 B6
Claydon 15 G2
Claypole 19 G2
Clayton 8 B5
Clayton West 24 A4
Clayton-le-Moors 23 E3
Clayton-le-Woods 22 D3
Cleadale 38 B6
Cleadon 29 E2
Cleator Moor 27 F5
Cleckheaton 24 A3
Cleehill 12 B1
Cleethorpes 25 G4
Clehonger 12 A3
Cleland 32 A3
Clenchwarton 20 C3
Clent 12 D1
Cleobury Mortimer 12 B1
Clevedon 12 A6
Cleveleys 22 C2
Cliffe 15 E6
Cliffe Woods 15 E6
Clitheroe 23 E2
Closeburn 27 E1
Cloughton 29 H6
Clova 37 E1
Clovelly 4 C2
Clovenfords 32 D4
Clovullin 35 F1
Clowne 24 B6
Clun 17 F6
Clunderwen 10 C4
Clunes 39 F6
Clungunford 12 A1
Clutton 6 B2
Clydach 11 E4
Clydach Vale 11 G5
Clydebank 31 H3
Clyro 11 H2
Coalburn 32 A4
Coalville 19 E4
Coast 39 E1
Coatbridge 32 A2
Cobham 8 B3
Cock Bridge 40 C5
Cockburnspath 33 F2
Cockenzie &
    Port Seton 32 D2
Cockerham 22 C2
Cockermouth 27 G4
Cockett 11 E5
Cockfield 28 D4
Coddenham 15 G2
Coddington 19 G2
Codicote 14 B4
Codnor 19 E2
Codsall 18 B4
Coggeshall 15 E3
Colchester 15 F3
Colden Common 7 F3
Coldingham 33 F2
Coldstream 33 F4
Coleford 12 B4
Colehill 6 D4
Coleshill 18 D5
Colintraive 31 F2
Colliston 41 G4
Collin 27 F2
Collingham 24 D6
Colmonell 26 D2
Colnabaichin 40 C5
Colnbrook 14 A6
Colne 23 E2
Colney Heath 14 B4
Colquhar 32 D3
Colsterworth 19 H3
Coltishall 21 F4
Colwich 18 C3
Colwick 19 F2
Colwyn Bay 16 D2
Colyford 5 G4
Colyton 5 G4

Combe Martin 4 D1
Combe St. Nicholas 5 G3
Comberton 14 C2
Comrie 36 B3
Congdon's Shop 4 B5
Congleton 23 E6
Congresbury 12 A6
Coningsby 20 A2
Conisbrough 24 C5
Coniston 27 H6
Connah's Quay 22 B6
Connel 35 F3
Conon Bridge 39 H3
Consett 28 D3
Constantine 3 G5
Contin 39 G3
Conwy 16 D2
Cookham 13 H5
Cookley 18 B5
Coombe Bissett 7 E3
Copley 28 C4
Copplestone 5 E3
Coppull 22 D4
Copythorne 7 F4
Corbridge 28 C2
Corby 19 G5
Corfe Castle 6 D5
Corfe Mullen 6 D5
Cornhill 4 B5
Cornhill-on-Tweed 33 F4
Cornholme 23 F3
Corpach 35 E3
Corrie 31 E4
Corringham 15 E5
Corsham 12 C6
Corsock 27 E2
Corton 21 H5
Corwen 17 E3
Coryton 15 E5
Cosby 19 F5
Coshieville 36 B2
Cotgrave 19 F3
Cottenham 14 C1
Cottesmore 19 H4
Cottingham ERid 25 E3
Cottingham
    N'hants 19 G5
Coulport 31 F2
Coundon 28 D4
Coupar Angus 36 D2
Cove A&B 31 F2
Cove High 38 D1
Cove Bay 41 G5
Coventry 13 F1
Coverack 3 G6
Cowbit 20 A4
Cowbridge 11 G6
Cowdenbeath 32 C1
Cowes 7 F5
Cowfold 8 B4
Cowie 32 A1
Cowling 23 F2
Cowshill 28 B3
Coxheath 9 E3
Coxwold 24 C1
Coychurch 11 G6
Coylton 31 G6
Coylumbridge 40 B5
Cradley 12 C2
Craichie 37 E2
Craig 39 F3
Craigandaive 31 E2
Craigdarroch 31 H6
Craigellachie 40 C3
Craigendoran 31 G2
Craighat 31 G2
Craignure 35 E3
Crail 37 F4
Cramlington 28 D2
Cramond 32 C2
Cranage 23 E6
Cranfield 14 A2
Cranleigh 8 A4

Cranshaws 33 E2
Cranwell 19 H2
Crask Inn 42 D4
Craster 33 H4
Crathie 40 C6
Craven Arms 17 G6
Crawfordjohn 32 A4
Crawley 8 B4
Creagorry 44 B7
Credenhill 12 A2
Crediton 5 E3
Creetown 26 C3
Cregneash 26 B6
Creswell 24 C6
Crewe 18 B2
Crewkerne 6 A4
Crianlarich (A' Chrion-
    Làraich) 35 H3
Criccieth 16 B4
Crickhowell 11 H4
Cricklade 12 D5
Crieff 36 B3
Crigglestone 24 B4
Crimond 41 G3
Crinan 30 D2
Cringleford 21 F4
Cripp's Corner 9 E4
Crocketford
    (Ninemile Bar) 27 E2
Croeserw 11 F5
Crofton 24 B4
Crofty 11 E5
Croick 39 G1
Cromarty 40 A2
Cromer 21 F2
Cromford 18 D2
Cromhall 12 B5
Crondall 7 H2
Crook 28 D4
Crookham 33 G4
Crosbost 44 E3
Crosby Mersey 22 C5
Crosby NLincs 24 D4
Crosby
    Ravensworth 28 A5
Cross Inn 11 E1
Crossaig 30 D4
Crosscanonby 27 F4
Crossford Fife 32 B1
Crossford SLan 32 A3
Crossgates Fife 32 C1
Crossgates
    Powys 11 G1
Crosshands 31 G5
Crosshill 31 G6
Crosshouse 31 G5
Crossmichael 27 E2
Crossway 11 G2
Croston 22 C4
Croughton 13 G3
Crow Hill 12 B3
Crowborough 8 D4
Crowland 20 A4
Crowle 24 D4
Crowthorne 13 H6
Croy High 40 A3
Croy NLan 32 A2
Croyde 4 C2
Croydon 14 C6
Cruden Bay 41 G4
Crumlin 11 H5
Crymych 10 C3
Crynant 11 F4
Cubbington 13 F1
Cuckfield 8 C4
Cuddington 22 D6
Cudworth 24 B4
Cuffley 14 C4
Culbokie 39 H3
Culcheth 22 D5
Culdrain 41 E4
Cullen 41 E2
Cullicudden 39 H2

Cullingworth 23 F3
Cullipool 30 D1
Cullivoe 45 J1
Cullompton 5 F3
Culmstock 5 F3
Culnacraig 42 A5
Culnaknock 38 C2
Culross 32 B1
Cults 41 F5
Cumbernauld 32 A2
Cuminestown 41 F3
Cumnock 31 H5
Cumnor 13 F4
Cunningsburgh 45 H5
Cupar 37 E4
Curry Rivel 6 A3
Cwm 11 H4
Cwmafan 11 F5
Cwmbrân 11 H5
Cwmllynfell 11 F4
Cymmer 11 G5
Cynghordy 11 F3
Cynwyl Elfed 10 D3

D

Dacre 27 H4
Dagenham 14 C5
Dailly 31 F6
Dairsie 37 E4
Dalabrog 44 B8
Dalbeattie 27 E2
Dalby 26 B6
Dale 10 A4
Dalgety Bay 32 C1
Dalham 15 E1
Dalkeith 32 D2
Dallas 40 C3
Dalmally 35 G3
Dalmellington 31 G6
Dalnavie 39 H2
Dalry 31 G4
Dalrymple 31 G6
Dalston 27 H3
Dalton 24 B5
Dalton-in-Furness 22 B1
Dalwhinnie 39 H6
Damerham 7 E4
Danbury 15 E4
Danby 29 G5
Danehill 8 C4
Darfield 24 B4
Darlington 28 D5
Darra 41 F3
Dartford 14 D6
Dartington 5 E5
Dartmeet 4 D5
Dartmouth 5 E6
Darton 24 B4
Darvel 31 H5
Darwen 22 D3
Dava 40 B4
Davenham 22 D6
Daventry 13 G1
Daviot 40 A4
Dawlish 5 F5
Deal 9 H3
Dearham 27 F4
Debenham 15 G2
Dechmont 32 B2
Deddington 13 F3
Dedham 15 F3
Deeping St. James 20 A4
Deeping
    St. Nicholas 20 A4
Deganwy 16 D2
Delabole 3 H2
Delamere 22 D6
Denbigh 22 A6
Denby Dale 24 A4
Denham 14 A5
Denholm 33 E5
Denholme 23 F3

Denmead 7 G4
Dennington 15 G1
Denny 32 A1
Denton 23 F5
Denver 20 C4
Derby 19 E3
Dereham
    (East Dereham) 21 E4
Dersingham 20 C3
Dervaig 34 C2
Desborough 19 G5
Devil's Bridge 11 F1
Devizes 12 D6
Dewsbury 24 A3
Dhoon 26 C5
Dibden 7 F4
Didcot 13 G5
Dinas Powys 11 H6
Dingwall 39 H3
Dinnet 40 D6
Dinnington 24 C5
Dippen 30 D5
Dirleton 33 E1
Diss 21 F5
Distington 27 F4
Ditton 9 E3
Dobwalls 4 B5
Dochgarroch 39 H3
Docking 20 D3
Doddington 33 G4
Dodington 12 C5
Dodworth 24 B4
Dogdyke 20 A2
Dolanog 17 E5
Dolbenmaen 16 C3
Dolfor 17 F6
Dolgarrog 16 D2
Dolgellau 16 D5
Dollar 32 B1
Dolphinton 32 C3
Doncaster 24 C4
Donington 20 A3
Donnington 18 A4
Dorchester 6 B5
Dordon 18 D4
Dores 39 H4
Dorking 8 B3
Dornie 38 D4
Dornoch 40 A1
Dougarie 30 D5
Douglas IoM 26 C6
Douglas SLan 32 A4
Douglastown 37 E2
Dounby 45 B2
Doune 36 B4
Dounreay 43 F2
Dover 9 H3
Doveridge 18 D3
Dowally 36 C2
Downham Market 20 C4
Downton 7 E3
Dowsby 20 A3
Drayton Norf 21 F4
Drayton Oxon 13 F5
Drefach 11 E4
Dreghorn 31 G5
Drem 33 E2
Driffield 25 E2
Drimnin 34 D2
Droitwich Spa 12 C1
Dronfield 24 B6
Drongan 31 G6
Droylsden 23 F5
Druid 17 E3
Druimdrishaig 30 D3
Drumbeg 42 B3
Drumclog 31 H5
Drumlithie 41 F6
Drummore 26 B4
Drumnadrochit 39 H4
Drybrook 12 B4
Drymen 31 G2
Duchally 42 C5

Duddo **33** G3
Dudley **18** C5
Duffield **19** E2
Dufftown **40** D3
Duirinish **38** D4
Dullingham **14** D2
Dulnain Bridge **40** B4
Dulverton **5** F2
Dumbarton **31** G3
Dumfries **27** E1
Dunbar **33** E2
Dunbeath **43** G4
Dunblane **36** B4
Dunchurch **13** F1
Dundee **37** E3
Dundonald **31** G5
Dundreggan **39** G5
Dundrennan **27** E3
Dunecht **41** F5
Dunfermline **32** B1
Dunholme **25** E6
Dunkeld **36** C2
Dunkirk **9** F3
Dunlop **31** G4
Dunnet **43** G1
Dunning **36** C4
Dunoon **31** F3
Dunragit **26** B3
Duns **33** F3
Dunscore **27** E1
Dunstable **14** A3
Dunster **5** F1
Dunure **31** F6
Dunvant **11** E5
Dunvegan **38** A3
Durham **28** D3
Durness **42** C2
Durrington **7** E2
Dursley **12** C5
Dyce **41** F5
Dyke **40** B3
Dykehead **37** E1
Dymchurch **9** F4
Dymock **12** C3
Dyserth **22** A6

E

Eaglescliffe **29** E5
Eaglesfield **27** G2
Eaglesham **31** H4
Ealing **14** B6
Earby **23** F2
Eardisley **12** A2
Earith **14** C1
Earl Shilton **19** E5
Earl Stonham **15** G2
Earls Barton **13** H1
Earls Colne **15** E3
Earlston **33** E4
Earsairidh **44** B10
Easebourne **7** H4
Easington *Dur* **29** E3
Easington *ERid* **25** G3
Easington Colliery **29** E3
Easingwold **24** C1
East Bergholt **15** F2
East Bridgford **19** F2
East Calder **32** B2
East Dereham
  (Dereham) **21** E4
East Goscote **19** F4
East Grinstead **8** C4
East Hanney **13** F5
East Harling **21** E5
East Haven **37** F3
East Horsley **6** A3
East Huntspill **6** A2
East Keal **25** G6
East Kilbride **31** H4
East Leake **19** F3
East Linton **33** E2
East Malling **9** E3

East Markham **24** D6
East Preston **8** A5
East Retford
  (Retford) **24** D5
East Wemyss **32** D1
East Wittering **7** H5
Eastbourne **8** D6
Easter Lednathie **37** E1
Eastfield **29** H6
Eastgate **28** C4
Eastleigh **7** F4
Eastoft **24** D4
Easton **6** B6
Easton on the Hill **19** H4
Easton-in-
  Gordano **12** B6
Eastriggs **27** G2
Eastry **9** G3
Eastwood **19** E2
Eaton Socon **14** B2
Ebbw Vale **11** H4
Ecclaw **33** F2
Ecclefechan **27** G2
Eccles **33** F3
Ecclesfield **24** B5
Eccleshall **18** B3
Eccleston **22** D4
Echt **41** F5
Eckford **33** F4
Eckington *Derbys* **24** B6
Eckington *Worcs* **12** D2
Edderton **40** A1
Eddleston **32** C3
Edenbridge **8** C3
Edenfield **23** E4
Edgworth **23** E4
Edinburgh **32** C2
Edlingham **33** H5
Edmundbyers **28** C3
Edwinstowe **24** C6
Edzell **37** F1
Egglescliffe **29** E5
Egham **14** A6
Eglingham **33** H5
Eglwys Fach **16** C6
Eglwyswrw **10** C3
Egremont **27** F5
Egton **29** G5
Einacleit **44** D3
Elgin **40** C2
Elgol **38** C5
Elham **9** G3
Elie **37** E4
Eling **7** F4
Elland **24** A3
Ellenabeich **30** D1
Ellesmere **28** A6
Ellesmere Port **22** C6
Ellingham **33** H4
Ellington **28** D1
Ellon **41** G4
Elloughton **25** E3
Elm **20** B4
Elmswell **15** F1
Elmton **24** C6
Elphin **42** B5
Elsdon **28** C1
Elsrickle **32** B3
Elstead **8** A3
Elstree **14** B5
Elswick **22** C3
Elton *Cambs* **19** H5
Elton *ChesW&C* **22** C6
Elvanfoot **32** B5
Elvington **24** D2
Ely *Cambs* **14** D1
Ely *Cardiff* **11** H6
Embleton **33** H4
Emsworth **7** H4
Enderby **19** F5
Endon **18** C2
Enfield **14** C5
Enstone **13** F3

Enterkinfoot **32** A5
Eoropaidh **44** F1
Epping **14** C4
Epsom **14** B6
Epworth **24** D4
Eriboll **42** C3
Eriswell **15** E1
Errogie **39** H4
Errol **36** D3
Esh Winning **28** D3
Esher **14** B6
Eskdalemuir **27** G1
Eston **29** F5
Eton **14** A6
Ettendge **39** H6
Ettington **13** E2
Ettrick **32** C5
Ettrickbridge **32** D4
Euxton **22** D4
Evanton **39** H2
Evercreech **6** B3
Evesham **12** D2
Ewell **14** B6
Ewhurst **8** A3
Exebridge **5** F2
Exeter **5** F4
Exminster **5** F4
Exmouth **5** F4
Eye *Peter* **20** A4
Eye *Suff* **15** G1
Eyemouth **33** G2
Eynsford **14** D6
Eynsham **13** F4

F

Failsworth **23** E4
Fair Oak **7** F4
Fairford **13** E4
Fairlie **31** F4
Fairlight **9** E5
Fakenham **21** E3
Falkirk **32** A2
Falkland **36** D4
Fallin **32** A1
Falmouth **3** G5
Falstone **28** B1
Fareham **7** G4
Faringdon **13** E4
Farington **22** D3
Farmborough **12** B6
Farnborough **7** H2
Farndon **19** G2
Farnham **7** H2
Farnham Royal **14** A5
Farnsfield **19** F2
Farnworth **23** E4
Farr **39** H4
Fauldhouse **32** B2
Faversham **15** F6
Fawley **7** F4
Fazeley **18** D4
Fearnhead **22** D5
Fearnmore **38** D2
Featherstone
  Staffs **18** C4
Featherstone
  WYorks **24** B4
Felindre **17** F6
Felixstowe **15** G3
Felling **28** D2
Felsted **14** D3
Felton **33** H5
Feltwell **20** D5
Feniton **5** G4
Fenstanton **14** C1
Fenwick *EAyr* **31** G4
Fenwick *N'umb* **33** G3
Feochaig **30** D6
Feolin Ferry **30** B3
Fern **37** E1
Ferndale **11** G5
Ferndown **6** D4

Ferness **40** B3
Fernhill Heath **12** C2
Fernhurst **7** H3
Ferryden **37** G2
Ferryhill **28** D4
Feshiebridge **40** A5
Fettercairn **37** F1
Ffestiniog **16** D3
Ffostrasol **10** D2
Filey **25** F1
Fillongley **18** D5
Filton **12** B6
Fimber **24** D1
Finavon **37** E2
Finchampstead **13** H6
Finchingfield **14** D3
Findern **19** E3
Findhorn **40** B2
Findochty **40** D2
Findon **8** B5
Finedon **14** A1
Finningham **15** F1
Finningley **24** C5
Finnygaud **41** E3
Finstown **45** C3
Fintry **31** H2
Fionnphort **34** C3
Fishburn **29** E4
Fishguard
  (Abergwaun) **10** B3
Fishnish **34** D2
Fiunary **34** D2
Five Oaks **5** H6
Flackwell Heath **13** H5
Flamborough **25** F1
Fleet **7** H2
Fleetwood **22** C2
Flempton **15** E1
Flimby **27** F3
Flimwell **9** E4
Flint (Y Fflint) **22** B6
Flitwick **14** A3
Flodden **33** G4
Flookburgh **22** C1
Fochabers **40** D3
Folkestone **9** G4
Folkingham **19** H3
Folly Gate **4** D3
Ford *A&B* **30** D1
Ford *N'umb* **33** G4
Fordham **14** D1
Fordingbridge **7** E3
Fordoun **37** G1
Fordyce **41** E2
Forest Row **8** C4
Forfar **37** E2
Forgandenny **36** C4
Forgie **40** D3
Formby **22** B4
Forres **40** B3
Forsbrook **18** C2
Forsinard **43** E3
Fort Augustus **39** G5
Fort William
  (An Gearasdan) **35** G1
Forth **32** B3
Fortingall **36** B2
Fortrose **40** A3
Fortuneswell **6** B6
Fotherby **25** F5
Foulden **33** G3
Foulridge **23** E2
Four Elms **8** C3
Four Marks **7** G3
Four Oaks **9** E5
Fowey **4** B6
Fownhope **12** B3
Foxdale **26** B3
Foyers **39** G4
Framfield **8** C4
Framlingham **15** G1
Frampton
  Cotterell **12** B5

Frampton on
  Severn **12** C4
Frankley **18** C5
Fraserburgh **41** G2
Freckleton **22** C3
Fremington **4** D2
Freshwater **7** F5
Freshwater East **10** B5
Fressingfield **15** G1
Freswick **43** H2
Freuchie **36** D4
Fridaythorpe **24** D2
Frimley **7** H2
Frinton-on-Sea **15** G4
Friockheim **37** F2
Frithelstock Stone **4** C3
Frizington **27** F5
Frodsham **22** D3
Frogmore **7** H2
Frome **6** C2
Fulbourn **14** D2
Fulford *Staffs* **18** C3
Fulford *York* **24** C2
Fulham **14** B6
Fulwood **22** D3
Furnace **31** E1
Fyfield **14** D4
Fyvie **41** F4

G

Gaer **11** H3
Gainford **28** D5
Gainsborough **24** D5
Gairloch **38** D2
Galashiels **32** D4
Galmisdale **38** B6
Galston **31** H5
Gamlingay **14** B2
Gardenstown **41** F2
Garelochhead **31** F2
Garforth **24** B3
Gargrave **23** F2
Garlieston **26** C3
Garsdale Head **28** B6
Garstang **22** C2
Garth **11** G2
Garthmyl **17** F6
Gartocharn **31** G2
Garvald **33** E2
Garvamore **39** H6
Garvard **30** B2
Garve **39** G2
Gatehouse of Fleet **26** D3
Gateshead **28** D2
Gatley **23** E5
Gawthrop **28** A6
Gayton **20** D4
Geddington **19** G5
Gedney **20** B3
Gelligaer **11** H5
Georgeham **4** C2
Gerrards Cross **14** A5
Giffnock **31** H4
Gifford **33** E2
Gilberdyke **24** D3
Gillamoor **29** F6
Gilling West **28** D5
Gillingham *Dorset* **6** C3
Gillingham *Med* **15** E6
Gilmerton **36** B3
Gilsland **28** A2
Gilston **32** D3
Gilwern **11** H4
Girvan **26** B1
Gisburn **23** E2
Glamis **37** E2
Glanaman **11** E4
Glanton **33** G5
Glasbury **11** H3
Glasgow **31** H3
Glassford **32** A3
Glastonbury **6** B3

Glemsford 15 E2
Glen Vine 26 C6
Glenbarr 30 C5
Glenbeg 34 D1
Glenborrodale 34 D1
Glenbreck 32 B4
Glenbrittle 38 B4
Glencaple 27 F2
Glencarse 36 D3
Glencoe 35 G2
Gleneagles 36 C4
Glenegedale 30 B4
Glenelg 38 D5
Glenfarg 36 D4
Glenfield 19 F4
Glenfinnan 39 E6
Glengarnock 31 G4
Glenkindie 40 D5
Glenluce 26 B3
Glenrothes 36 D4
Glinton 20 A4
Glossop 23 F5
Gloucester 12 C4
Glusburn 23 F2
Glyn Ceiriog 17 F4
Glyncorrwg 11 F5
Glyn-Neath 11 F4
Gnosall 18 B3
Gobowen 17 F4
Godalming 8 A3
Godmanchester 14 B1
Godstone 8 C3
Golborne 22 D5
Goldcliff 12 A5
Golden Pot 7 H2
Golspie 40 A1
Goodwick 10 B3
Goole 24 D3
Goonhavern 3 G4
Gordon 33 E3
Gorebridge 32 D2
Gorey 5 H6
Goring 13 G5
Gorseinon 11 E5
Gosberton 20 A3
Gosfield 15 E3
Gosforth Cumb 27 F5
Gosforth T&W 28 D2
Gosport 7 G5
Gotham 19 F3
Goudhurst 9 E4
Gourdon 37 G1
Goxhill 25 F3
Grabhair 44 E4
Grain 15 E6
Grampound 3 H4
Grandtully 36 C2
Grangemouth 32 B1
Grange-over-Sands 22 C1
Grantham 19 F1
Grantown-on-Spey 40 B4
Grantshouse 33 F2
Grasmere 27 F6
Grassington 23 F1
Gravesend 14 D6
Grayrigg 28 A6
Grays 14 D6
Grayshott 7 H3
Greasby 22 B5
Great Ayton 29 F5
Great Baddow 15 E4
Great Barton 15 E1
Great Bircham 20 D3
Great Broughton 29 F5
Great Clifton 27 F4
Great Cornard 15 E2
Great Dunmow 14 D3
Great Eccleston 22 C2
Great Ellingham 21 E5
Great Glen 19 F5
Great Gonerby 19 G3
Great Gransden 14 B2
Great Harwood 23 E3

Great Horkesley 15 F3
Great Linford 13 H2
Great Malvern 12 C2
Great Marton 22 C3
Great Missenden 13 H4
Great Notley 15 E3
Great Ponton 19 H3
Great Salkeld 28 A4
Great Sampford 15 E2
Great Sankey 22 D5
Great Shelford 14 C2
Great Torrington 4 D3
Great Wakering 15 F5
Great Wyrley 18 C4
Great Yarmouth 21 H4
Great Yeldham 15 E3
Greatham 7 H3
Greatstone-on-Sea 9 F4
Greengairs 32 A2
Greenham 13 F6
Greenhead 28 A2
Greenlaw 33 F3
Greenloaning 36 B4
Greenock 31 F3
Greenodd 27 H6
Greenway 10 B3
Greenwich 14 C6
Gresford 17 G3
Gress 44 E2
Gretna 27 H2
Greystoke 27 H4
Grimoldby 25 G5
Grimsby 25 F4
Grimston 20 D3
Gringley on the
  Hill 24 D5
Grizebeck 27 G6
Grove 13 F5
Grudie 39 G2
Guide Post 28 D1
Guildford 8 A3
Guildtown 36 D3
Guisborough 29 F5
Guiseley 24 A2
Guist 21 E3
Gullane 32 D1
Gunness 24 E4
Gunnislake 4 C5
Gurnos 11 F4
Gutcher 45 J2
Gwaun-Cae-
  Gurwen 11 F4
Gwithian 3 F4
Gwytherin 16 D2

H

Hackleton 13 H2
Hacklinge 9 H3
Hackness 29 H6
Haddenham 14 C1
Haddington 33 E2
Haddiscoe 21 G5
Hadleigh 15 F2
Hadley 18 A4
Hagley Here 12 B2
Hagley Worcs 18 C5
Hailsham 8 D5
Hale 23 E5
Hales 21 G5
Halesowen 18 C5
Halesworth 15 H1
Halewood 22 C5
Halifax 23 F3
Halkirk 43 G3
Halkyn 22 B6
Hall 31 G4
Halland 8 D5
Hallow 12 C2
Hallworthy 4 B4
Halstead 15 E3
Halton Gill 23 E1
Haltwhistle 28 B2

Halwell 5 E6
Ham 45 F5
Hamble-le-Rice 7 F4
Hambleton 22 C2
Hamilton 32 A3
Hamnavoe 45 H5
Hampreston 6 D5
Hamstreet 9 F4
Handsacre 18 C4
Hanham 12 B6
Hanley Castle 12 C2
Hanwood 17 G5
Happisburgh 21 G3
Harbledown 9 G3
Harbost 44 F1
Harbury 13 F2
Hardingstone 13 H2
Hardwicke 12 C4
Hare Street 14 C3
Harefield 14 A5
Harewood 24 B2
Harlech 16 C4
Harleston 21 F5
Harlington 14 A3
Harlow 14 C4
Harmston 25 E6
Haroldswick 45 J1
Harpenden 14 B4
Harpole 13 G1
Harrietfield 36 C3
Harrietsham 9 E3
Harrogate 24 B2
Harrow 14 B5
Harston 14 C2
Hartfield 8 C4
Harthill 32 B2
Hartland 4 B2
Hartlebury 12 C1
Hartlepool 29 F4
Hartley 14 D6
Hartley Wintney 7 H2
Hartpury 12 C3
Hartshill 19 E5
Hartshorne 19 E3
Harvington 12 D2
Harwell 13 F5
Harwich 15 G3
Harworth 24 C5
Hasland 24 B6
Haslemere 8 A4
Haslingden 23 E3
Hassendean 33 E4
Hastings 9 E5
Haswell 29 E3
Hatfield Herts 14 B4
Hatfield SYorks 24 C4
Hatfield Broad Oak 14 D4
Hatfield Peverel 15 E4
Hatherleigh 4 D3
Hathern 19 E3
Hathersage 24 A5
Hatton Aber 41 G4
Hatton Derbys 18 D3
Haugh of Urr 27 E2
Haughton 18 B3
Havant 7 H4
Haverfordwest
  (Hwlffordd) 10 B3
Haverhill 14 D2
Hawarden
  (Penarlâg) 17 G3
Hawes 28 B6
Hawick 33 E5
Hawkhurst 9 E4
Hawkinge 9 G3
Hawkshead 27 H6
Hawkwell 15 E5
Hawley 7 H2
Haworth 23 F3
Haxby 24 C2
Haxey 24 D5
Haydock 22 D5
Haydon Bridge 28 B2

Haydon Wick 13 E5
Hayfield 23 F5
Hayle 3 F5
Hay-on-Wye 11 H2
Hayton 24 D2
Haywards Heath 8 C4
Hazel Grove 23 F5
Hazlemere 13 H5
Heacham 20 C3
Headcorn 9 E3
Headley 7 H3
Healeyfield 28 C3
Healing 25 F4
Heanor 19 E2
Heath 24 B6
Heathfield 8 D4
Hebburn 29 E2
Hebden Bridge 23 F3
Heckington 20 A2
Hedge End 7 F4
Hedon 25 F3
Heighington 25 E6
Helensburgh 31 F2
Helhoughton 20 D3
Hellifield 23 E2
Helmsdale 43 F5
Helmsley 29 F6
Helpringham 20 A2
Helsby 22 C6
Helston 3 F5
Hemel Hempstead 14 A4
Hemingford Grey 14 B1
Hempnall 21 F5
Hempstead 14 D3
Hemsby 21 G4
Hemsworth 24 B4
Hemyock 5 G3
Hendon 14 B5
Henfield 8 B5
Hengoed 11 H5
Henley-in-Arden 13 E1
Henley-on-
  Thames 13 H5
Henlow 14 B3
Henstridge 6 C4
Hereford 12 B2
Heriot 32 D3
Herne Bay 15 G6
Herstmonceux 8 D5
Hertford 14 C4
Heswall 22 B5
Hethersett 21 F4
Hetton 23 F2
Hetton-le-Hole 29 E3
Hexham 28 C2
Hextable 14 D6
Heybridge 15 E4
Heysham 22 C1
Heywood 23 E4
Hibaldstow 25 E4
High Bentham 22 D1
High Blantyre 31 H4
High Bradfield 24 A5
High Etherley 28 D4
High Garrett 15 E3
High Halden 9 E4
High Hawsker 29 H5
High Hesket 27 H3
High Legh 23 E5
High Lorton 27 G4
High Wycombe 13 H5
Higham 15 E6
Higham Ferrers 14 A1
Highampton 4 C3
Highbridge 6 A2
Highclere 13 F6
Higher Walton 22 D3
Highley 18 B5
Highnam 12 C4
Highworth 13 E5
Hildenborough 8 D3
Hilgay 20 C5
Hill End 32 B1

Hill of Fearn 40 A2
Hillingdon 14 A5
Hillside 37 G1
Hillswick 45 G3
Hilperton 6 C2
Hilton 18 D3
Hinckley 19 E5
Hinderwell 29 G5
Hindhead 7 H3
Hindley 22 D4
Hindon 6 D3
Hingham 21 E4
Hirwaun 11 G4
Histon 14 C1
Hitchin 14 B3
Hockley 15 E5
Hockley Heath 13 E1
Hoddesdon 14 C4
Hodnet 18 A3
Hogsthorpe 25 H6
Holbeach 20 B3
Holbrook 15 G3
Holden 23 E2
Holland-on-Sea 15 G4
Hollington 9 E5
Hollingworth 23 F5
Hollybush EAyr 31 G6
Hollybush Worcs 12 C3
Holme-on-Spalding-
  Moor 24 D3
Holmes Chapel 23 E6
Holmesfield 24 B6
Holmfirth 24 A4
Holsworthy 4 C3
Holt Norf 21 E3
Holt Wilts 12 C6
Holt Wrex 17 G3
Holyhead
  (Caergybi) 16 A1
Holywell 22 B6
Holywood 27 F1
Homersfield 21 F5
Honiton 5 G3
Honley 24 A4
Hoo 15 E6
Hook ERid 24 D3
Hook Hants 7 H2
Hook Norton 13 F3
Hope 17 G3
Hopeman 40 C2
Hopton Norf 21 H4
Hopton Suff 15 F1
Horam 8 D5
Horbling 20 A3
Horbury 24 A4
Horden 29 E3
Horeb 10 D2
Horley 8 B3
Hornby 22 D4
Horncastle 25 F6
Horndean 7 H4
Horning 21 G4
Hornsea 25 F2
Horrabridge 4 D5
Horringer 15 E1
Horsehouse 28 C6
Horsford 21 F4
Horsham 8 A3
Horsmonden 9 E4
Horstead 21 F4
Horton Heath 7 F4
Horton in
  Ribblesdale 23 E1
Horwich 22 D4
Hoswick 45 H5
Houghton le Spring 29 E3
Houghton Regis 14 A3
Houndslow 33 E3
Hounslow 14 B6
Houston 31 G3
Houton 45 C3
Hove 8 B5

Hoveton 21 G4
Hovingham 24 C1
Howden 24 D3
Howwood 31 G3
Hoylake 22 B5
Hoyland 24 B4
Hucknall 19 F2
Huddersfield 24 A4
Huggate 24 D2
Hugh Town 3 F3
Huish Episcopi 6 A3
Huisinis 44 C4
Hull 25 F3
Hullavington 12 C5
Hullbridge 15 E5
Humberston 25 G4
Humbie 32 D2
Hundleby 25 G6
Hundleton 10 B4
Hungerford 13 F6
Hunmanby 25 F1
Hunstanton 20 C2
Hunter's Quay 31 F3
Huntingdon 14 B1
Huntly 41 E3
Hurlford 31 G5
Hursley 7 F3
Hurst Green 9 E4
Hurstbourne Tarrant 7 F2
Hurstpierpoint 8 B5
Hurworth-on-Tees 29 E5
Husbands
  Bosworth 19 F5
Huttoft 25 H6
Hutton Cranswick 25 E2
Hutton Rudby 29 E5
Huyton 22 C5
Hyde 23 F5
Hythe Hants 7 F4
Hythe Kent 9 G4

I

Ibstock 19 E4
Icklesham 9 E5
Icklingham 15 E1
Idrigil 38 B3
Ilchester 6 B3
Ilford 14 C5
Ilfracombe 4 D1
Ilkeston 19 E2
Ilkley 24 A2
Ilminster 6 A4
Immingham 25 F3
Inchbare 37 F1
Inchnadamph 42 B4
Inchture 36 D3
Ingatestone 14 D5
Ingleton Dur 28 D4
Ingleton NYorks 22 D1
Inglewhite 22 D2
Ingoldmells 25 H6
Inkberrow 12 D2
Innellan 31 F3
Innerleithen 32 D4
Insch 41 E4
Inveralligan 38 D3
Inverallochy 41 G2
Inveraray 31 E1
Inverarity 37 E2
Inverarnan 31 G1
Inverbervie 37 G1
Invercassley 42 C5
Invercharnan 35 G2
Inverey 40 B6
Invergarry 39 G5
Invergordon 40 A2
Inverinan 31 E1
Inverkeilor 37 F2
Inverkeithing 32 C1
Inverkirkaig 42 A5
Inverlael 39 F1
Invermoriston 39 G5

Inverneil 30 D2
Inverness
  (Inbhir Nis) 39 H3
Invernoaden 31 F2
Inverurie 41 F4
Ipplepen 5 E5
Ipstones 18 C2
Ipswich 15 G2
Irchester 14 A1
Irlam 23 E5
Ironbridge 18 A4
Irthlingborough 14 A1
Irvine 31 G5
Isle of Whithorn 26 C4
Isleham 14 D1
Iver 14 A5
Ivinghoe 14 A4
Ivybridge 4 D6
Iwade 15 F6
Ixworth 15 F1

J

Jarrow 29 E2
Jaywick 15 G4
Jedburgh 33 E4
Jemimaville 40 A2
John o' Groats 43 H2
Johnston 10 B4
Johnstone 31 G3
Johnstonebridge 27 F1

K

Kames 31 E3
Kearsley 23 E4
Kedington 15 E2
Keelby 25 F4
Keele 18 B2
Kegworth 19 E3
Keighley 23 F2
Keillmore 30 C2
Keiss 43 H2
Keith 40 D3
Kellas Angus 37 E3
Kellas Moray 40 C3
Kelso 33 F4
Kelty 32 C1
Kelvedon 15 E4
Kelvedon Hatch 14 D5
Kemnay 41 F5
Kempsey 12 C2
Kempston 14 A2
Kendal 28 A6
Kenilworth 13 E1
Kenknock 35 H3
Kenmore 36 B2
Kennacraig 30 D3
Kennethmont 41 E4
Kennington 13 G4
Kennoway 37 E4
Kensaleyre 38 B3
Kensworth 14 A4
Kentallen 35 F2
Kenton 5 F4
Keoldale 42 C2
Kesgrave 15 G2
Kessingland 21 H5
Keswick 27 G4
Kettering 13 H1
Kettlewell 23 F1
Ketton 19 H4
Kewstoke 12 A6
Keyingham 25 F3
Keymer 8 C5
Keynsham 12 B6
Keyworth 19 F3
Kibworth Harcourt 19 F5
Kidderminster 12 C1
Kidlington 13 F4
Kidsgrove 18 B2
Kidwelly 10 D4
Kielder 28 A1

Kilberry 30 D3
Kilbirnie 31 G4
Kilburn 19 E2
Kilcadzow 32 A3
Kilchenzie 30 C5
Kilchiaran 30 A4
Kilchoan 34 C1
Kilchoman 30 A3
Kilchrenan 35 F3
Kilconquhar 37 E4
Kilcreggan 31 F2
Kildonan Lodge 43 F4
Kildrummy 40 D5
Kilfinan 31 E3
Kilgetty 10 C4
Kilham ERid 25 E1
Kilham N'umb 33 F4
Kilkhampton 4 B3
Killamarsh 24 B5
Killay 11 E5
Killean 30 C4
Killearn 31 H2
Killichonan 36 A2
Killiecrankie 36 C1
Killin 36 A3
Killinghall 24 A2
Killingworth 28 D2
Killundine 34 D2
Kilmacolm 31 G3
Kilmalieu 35 E2
Kilmaluag 38 B2
Kilmarnock 31 G5
Kilmartin 30 D2
Kilmaurs 31 G4
Kilmelford 30 D1
Kilmington 6 B4
Kilmory A&B 30 D3
Kilmory High 38 B5
Kilninian 34 C2
Kilninver 35 E3
Kiloran 30 B2
Kilrenny 37 F4
Kilsyth 32 A2
Kilwinning 31 G4
Kimberley Norf 21 E4
Kimberley Notts 19 F2
Kimbolton 14 B1
Kimpton 14 B4
Kinbrace 43 E4
Kincardine 32 B1
Kincardine O'Neil 41 E6
Kincraig 40 A5
Kingarth 31 E4
Kinghorn 32 C1
Kinglassie 32 C1
Kings Langley 14 A4
King's Lynn 20 C3
King's Sutton 13 F3
Kings Worthy 7 F3
Kingsbarns 37 F4
Kingsbridge 5 E6
Kingsbury 18 D5
Kingsbury Episcopi 6 A3
Kingsclere 7 G2
Kingsdown 9 H3
Kingshouse 36 A3
Kingskerswell 5 E5
Kingsley
  ChesW&C 22 D6
Kingsley Staffs 18 C2
Kingsnorth 9 F4
Kingsteignton 5 E5
Kingsthorne 12 B3
Kingston 40 D2
Kingston Bagpuize 13 F5
Kingston Seymour 12 A6
Kingston upon
  Hull 25 F3
Kingston upon
  Thames 14 B6
Kingstone 12 A3
Kingswear 5 E6
Kingswood SGlos 12 B6

Kingswood Surr 8 B3
Kington 11 H2
Kingussie 40 A5
Kinloch 38 B6
Kinloch Hourn 39 E5
Kinloch Rannoch 36 A2
Kinlochard 31 G1
Kinlochbervie 42 B3
Kinlocheil 35 F1
Kinlochewe 39 E2
Kinlochleven 35 G1
Kinloss 40 B2
Kinmel Bay 22 A5
Kinross 32 C1
Kintbury 13 F6
Kintore 41 F5
Kintour 30 B4
Kintra 30 B4
Kinver 18 B5
Kippax 24 B3
Kippen 31 H2
Kirby Muxloe 19 F4
Kirk Michael 26 C5
Kirk Sandall 24 C4
Kirk Yetholm 33 F4
Kirkbean 27 F3
Kirkbride 27 G3
Kirkburton 24 A4
Kirkby 22 C5
Kirkby in Ashfield 19 E2
Kirkby Lonsdale 22 D1
Kirkby Malzeard 24 A1
Kirkby Stephen 28 B5
Kirkbymoorside 29 F6
Kirkcaldy 32 C1
Kirkcolm 26 A2
Kirkconnel 32 A5
Kirkcowan 26 C2
Kirkcudbright 26 D3
Kirkham 22 C3
Kirkinner 26 C3
Kirkintilloch 31 H3
Kirkliston 32 C2
Kirkmichael P&K 36 C1
Kirkmichael SAyr 31 G6
Kirkmuirhill 32 A3
Kirknewton N'umb 33 G4
Kirknewton WLoth 32 C2
Kirkoswald Cumb 28 A3
Kirkoswald SAyr 31 F6
Kirkpatrick
  Durham 27 E2
Kirkpatrick-
  Fleming 27 G2
Kirkton 30 D1
Kirkton of
  Culsalmond 41 E4
Kirkton of Durris 41 F6
Kirkton of Glenisla 36 D1
Kirkton of
  Kingoldrum 37 E2
Kirkton of
  Menmuir 37 F1
Kirkton of Skene 41 F5
Kirktown of
  Auchterless 41 F3
Kirktown of
  Deskford 41 E2
Kirkwall 45 C3
Kirriemuir 37 E2
Kirtlington 13 F4
Kirton Lincs 20 B3
Kirton Suff 15 G3
Kirton in Lindsey 25 E5
Knaresborough 24 B2
Knayton 29 E6
Knebworth 14 B4
Knighton 11 H1
Knock 34 D3
Knockandhu 40 C4
Knottingley 24 C3
Knowle 13 E1
Knucklas 11 H1

Knutsford 23 E6
Kyle of Lochalsh (Caol
  Loch Aillse) 38 D4
Kyleakin 38 D4
Kylerhea 38 D4
Kyles Scalpay 44 D5
Kylestrome 42 B4

L

Laceby 25 F4
Lacock 12 D6
Ladybank 36 D4
Ladykirk 33 F3
Ladysford 41 G2
Lagg 31 E5
Laggan (Invergarry)
  High 39 F6
Laggan (Newtonmore)
  High 39 H6
Lagganulva 34 C2
Laide 38 D1
Lairg 42 D5
Lakenheath 20 D5
Laleston 11 F6
Lamberhurst 8 C4
Lambourn 13 F6
Lamlash 31 E5
Lampeter 11 E2
Lamport 13 H1
Lanark 32 A3
Lancaster 22 C1
Lanchester 28 D3
Landore 11 E5
Lane End 13 H5
Langford 14 B2
Langham 19 G4
Langholm 27 H1
Langold 24 C5
Langport 6 A3
Langtoft 25 E1
Langwathby 28 A4
Lanivet 3 H3
Lapworth 13 E1
Larbert 32 A1
Largoward 37 E4
Largs 31 F4
Larkhall 32 A3
Larkhill 7 E2
Larling 21 E5
Latchingdon 15 E4
Latheron 43 G4
Latheronwheel 43 G4
Lauder 33 E3
Laugharne 10 D4
Launceston 4 C3
Laurencekirk 37 G1
Laurieston 26 D2
Lavenham 15 F2
Law 32 A3
Lawers 36 A3
Lawford 15 F3
Laxey 26 C5
Laxford Bridge 42 B3
Layer de la Haye 15 F4
Lazonby 28 A4
Leadburn 32 C3
Leadenham 19 H2
Leadgate 28 D3
Leadhills 32 A5
Leamington Spa 13 F1
Leasingham 19 H2
Leatherhead 8 B3
Leavening 24 D1
Lechlade-on-
  Thames 13 E5
Leckhampton 12 D4
Leckmelm 39 F1
Ledaig 35 F3
Ledbury 12 C3
Ledmore 42 B5
Lee 22 D2
Lee Moor 4 D5

Leeds 24 A3
Leedstown 3 F5
Leek 18 C2
Leeming 28 D6
Lee-on-the-Solent 7 G4
Leicester 19 F4
Leigh 22 D4
Leighton Buzzard 14 A3
Leiston 15 H1
Leith 32 C2
Lenham 9 E3
Lennoxtown 31 H3
Leominster 12 A2
Lerwick 45 H4
Lesbury 33 H5
Leslie 36 D4
Lesmahagow 32 A4
Leswalt 26 A2
Letchworth Garden
  City 14 B3
Letheringsett 21 E3
Letterston 10 B3
Leuchars 37 E3
Leumrabhagh 44 E4
Leven ERid 25 F2
Leven Fife 37 E4
Levenwick 45 H5
Leverburgh 44 C5
Lewes 8 C5
Lewisham 14 C6
Leyburn 28 D6
Leyland 22 D3
Leysdown-on-Sea 15 F6
Lhanbryde 40 C2
Libberton 32 B3
Lichfield 18 D4
Lightwater 14 A6
Lilleshall 18 B4
Lilliesleaf 33 E4
Limekilns 32 B1
Lincoln 25 E6
Lindfield 8 C4
Lindores 36 D4
Linford 14 D6
Lingfield 8 C3
Linksness 45 B3
Linlithgow 32 B2
Linsidemore 39 H1
Linton 13 D2
Liphook 7 H3
Liskeard 4 B5
Liss 7 H3
Liswerry 12 A5
Litherland 22 C5
Little Clacton 15 G4
Little Common 9 E5
Little Downham 20 C5
Little Eaton 19 E2
Little Missenden 14 A5
Little Oakley 15 G3
Little Paxton 14 B1
Little Plumstead 21 G4
Littleborough 23 F4
Littlebourne 9 G4
Littledean 12 B4
Littlehampton 8 A5
Littlemill EAyr 31 G2
Littlemill High 40 B3
Littlemore 13 G4
Littleport 20 C5
Littlestone-on-Sea 9 F4
Liverpool 22 C5
Liversedge 24 A3
Livingston 32 B2
Lizard 3 G6
Llanaelhaearn 16 B3
Llanarth 12 A4
Llanarthney 11 F3
Llanbadarn Fawr 16 C6
Llanbadrig 16 B1
Llanbedr 16 C4
Llanbedrog 16 B4
Llanberis 16 C2

Llanbister 11 H1
Llanblethian 11 G6
Llanddarog 11 E4
Llanddeiniolen 16 C2
Llandderfel 17 E4
Llanddowror 10 C4
Llandeilo 11 E3
Llandinam 17 E6
Llandissilio 10 C3
Llandovery
  (Llanymddyfri) 11 F3
Llandrillo 17 E4
Llandrindod Wells 11 G1
Llandudno 16 D1
Llandwrog 16 B3
Llandybie 11 E4
Llandysul 10 D2
Llanegwad 11 E3
Llanelli 11 E4
Llanelltyd 16 D5
Llanelly 11 H4
Llanfaelog 16 B2
Llanfair Caereinion 17 F5
Llanfair Talhaiarn 22 A6
Llanfairfechan 16 C2
Llanfairpwllgwyngyll
  16 C2
Llanfihangel
  ar-arth 10 D3
Llanfyllin 17 F5
Llanfynydd 17 F3
Llangadfan 17 E5
Llangadog 11 F3
Llangefni 16 B2
Llangeler 10 D3
Llangelynin 16 C5
Llangeindeirne 10 D4
Llangernyw 16 D2
Llangoed 16 C2
Llangollen 17 F3
Llangranog 10 D2
Llangunnor 10 D3
Llangurig 11 G1
Llangwm 10 B4
Llangynidr 11 H4
Llanharan 11 G5
Llanhilleth 11 H4
Llanidloes 17 E6
Llanilar 11 E1
Llanishen 11 H5
Llanllwchaiarn 17 F6
Llanllyfni 16 B3
Llannerch-y-medd 16 B1
Llannon 11 E4
Llanon 11 E1
Llanrhaeadr-ym-
  Mochnant 17 F4
Llanrhidian 11 E5
Llanrhystud 11 E1
Llanrug 16 C2
Llanrumney 11 H5
Llanrwst 16 D2
Llansamlet 11 E5
Llansanffraid Glan
  Conwy 16 D2
Llansannan 22 A6
Llansawel 11 E3
Llansteffan 10 D4
Llanthony 11 H3
Llantilio Pertholey 12 A3
Llantrisant Mon 12 A5
Llantrisant RCT 11 G5
Llantwit Major 11 G6
Llanuwchllyn 16 D4
Llanwddyn 17 E5
Llanwnda 16 B3
Llanwnog 17 E6
Llanwrda 11 F3
Llanwrtyd Wells 11 F2
Llanybydder 11 E2
Llanynghenedl 16 B1
Llanystumdwy 16 B4
Lledrod 11 E1

Loanhead 32 C2
Loans 31 G5
Loch Sgioport 44 B8
Lochailort 38 D6
Lochaline
  (Loch Àlainn) 34 D2
Lochans 26 A3
Lochcarron 38 D4
Lochcarron 35 D4
Lochdon 35 E3
Lochearnhead 36 A3
Lochend 39 H4
Lochgelly 32 C1
Lochgilphead 30 D2
Lochgoilhead 31 F1
Lochinver 42 A4
Lochmaben 27 F1
Lochmaddy (Loch na
  Madadh) 44 C6
Lochranza 31 E4
Lochwinnoch 31 G4
Lockerbie 27 G1
Locking 6 A2
Locks Heath 7 G4
Lockton 29 G6
Loddiswell 5 E6
Loddon 21 G5
Lofthouse 24 B3
Loftus 29 G5
Logan 31 H5
Loggerheads 18 B3
London 14 C5
London Colney 14 B4
Long Bennington 19 G2
Long Buckby 13 G1
Long Compton 13 E3
Long Crendon 13 G4
Long Eaton 19 E3
Long Hanborough 13 F4
Long Itchington 13 F1
Long Lawford 13 F1
Long Melford 15 E2
Long Preston 23 E2
Long Stratton 21 F5
Long Sutton Lincs 20 B3
Long Sutton Som 6 A3
Longbenton 28 D2
Longbridge Deverill 6 C2
Longdon 18 C4
Longforgan 37 E3
Longframlington 33 H5
Longhope Glos 12 B4
Longhope Ork 45 C4
Longhorsley 28 D1
Longhoughton 33 H5
Longmanhill 41 F2
Longmorn 40 C3
Longniddry 32 D2
Longridge 22 D3
Longside 41 G3
Longton 22 C3
Longtown 27 H2
Looe 4 B6
Loose 9 E3
Lopcombe Corner 7 E3
Loscoe 19 E2
Lossiemouth 40 C2
Lostwithiel 4 B6
Loth 45 D2
Lothmore 43 H5
Loughborough 19 F4
Loughor 11 E5
Loughton 14 C5
Louth 25 G5
Low Street 21 G3
Lowdham 19 F2
Lower Beeding 8 B4
Lower Cam 12 C4
Lower Diabaig 38 D2

Lower Killeyan 30 A4
Lowestoft 21 H5
Loweswater 27 G4
Lowick 33 G3
Ludag 44 B9
Ludgershall 7 E2
Ludgvan 3 F5
Ludlow 12 B1
Luib 38 C4
Lumphanan 41 E5
Luncarty 36 C3
Lundin Links 37 E4
Lunna 45 H3
Luss 31 G2
Lusta 38 A3
Luton 14 B3
Lutterworth 19 F5
Luxulyan 3 H4
Lybster 43 G4
Lydd 9 F4
Lydford 4 D4
Lydiate 22 C4
Lydney 12 B4
Lyme Regis 6 A5
Lyminge 9 G3
Lymington 7 F5
Lymm 22 D5
Lympne 9 G4
Lympstone 5 E4
Lyndhurst 7 F4
Lyne of Skene 41 F5
Lyneham 12 D6
Lynemore 40 B4
Lynemouth 28 D1
Lyness 45 C4
Lynmouth 5 E1
Lynton 5 E1
Lytchett Matravers 6 D5
Lytchett Minster 6 D5
Lytham
  St. Anne's 22 C3

M

Mablethorpe 25 H5
Macclesfield 23 F6
Macduff 41 F2
Macharioch 30 D6
Machen 11 H5
Machrihanish 30 C6
Machynlleth 16 D5
Macmerry 32 D2
Madeley 18 B2
Madley 12 A3
Madron 3 E5
Maenclochog 10 B3
Maentwrog 16 C3
Maerdy 11 G5
Maesteg 11 F5
Maghull 22 C4
Maiden Bradley 6 C3
Maiden Newton 6 B5
Maidenhead 13 H5
Maidens 31 F6
Maidstone 9 E3
Maldon 15 E4
Mallaig (Malaig) 38 C6
Mallwyd 16 D5
Malmesbury 12 D6
Malpas ChesW&C 17 G3
Malpas Newport 12 A5
Maltby 24 C5
Maltby le Marsh 25 G5
Malton 24 D1
Malvern Link 12 C2
Manby 25 G5
Mancetter 19 E5
Manchester 23 E5
Manea 20 B5
Mangotsfield 12 B6
Manningtree 15 G3
Manorbier 10 B5
Mansfield 24 C6

Mansfield
  Woodhouse 24 C6
Manston 6 C4
Marazion 3 F5
March 20 B5
Marchwiel 17 G3
Marden 9 E3
Mareham le Fen 25 F6
Maresfield 8 C4
Margam 11 F5
Margate 15 H6
Marham 20 D4
Mark 6 A2
Market Bosworth 19 E4
Market Deeping 20 A4
Market Drayton 18 A3
Market
  Harborough 19 G5
Market Lavington 6 D2
Market Rasen 25 F5
Market Warsop 24 C6
Markfield 19 E4
Markinch 36 D4
Marks Tey 15 F3
Markyate 14 A4
Marlborough 13 E6
Marldon 5 E5
Marlow 13 H5
Marnhull 6 C4
Marple 23 F4
Marsden 23 F4
Marshfield 12 C6
Marske-by-the-Sea 29 F4
Marston 13 G4
Marston Magna 6 B3
Marston
  Moretaine 14 A2
Martham 21 G4
Martlesham 15 G2
Martley 12 C1
Martock 6 A4
Marybank 39 G3
Marykirk 37 F1
Marypark 40 C4
Maryport 27 F4
Marywell 41 F6
Masham 28 D6
Matlock 24 B6
Matlock Bath 18 D2
Mauchline 31 H5
Maud 41 G3
Maughold 26 C5
Maybole 31 G6
Mayfield 18 D2
Mealsgate 27 G3
Meare 6 A2
Measham 19 E4
Medstead 7 G3
Meidrim 10 C3
Meigle 36 D2
Meikle Kilmory 31 E3
Meikleour 36 D3
Melbourn 14 C2
Melbourne 19 E3
Melksham 12 D6
Melmerby 28 A4
Melrose 33 E4
Melsonby 28 D5
Meltham 23 F4
Melton 15 G2
Melton Mowbray 19 G4
Melvaig 38 D1
Melvich 43 E2
Memsie 41 G2
Menai Bridge 16 C2
Menston 24 A2
Menstrie 32 A1
Mere 6 C3
Meriden 18 D5
Merthyr Tydfil 11 G4
Messingham 24 D4
Metfield 21 F5

Metheringham 25 E6
Methlick 41 F4
Methven 36 C3
Methwold 20 D5
Mevagissey 3 H4
Mexborough 24 B5
Mey 43 G2
Mickleton *Dur* 28 C4
Mickleton *Glos* 13 E2
Mid Ardlaw 41 G2
Mid Yell 45 J2
Middle Barton 13 F3
Middle Rasen 25 E5
Middleham 28 D6
Middlemarsh 6 B4
Middlesbrough 29 E4
Middlesmoor 23 F1
Middleton *GtMan* 23 E4
Middleton *Norf* 20 C4
Middleton Cheney 13 F2
Middleton Stoney 13 G3
Middleton-in-
  Teesdale 28 C4
Middleton-on-Sea 8 A6
Middleton-on-the-
  Wolds 25 E2
Middlewich 23 E6
Midhurst 7 H3
Midlem 33 E4
Midsomer Norton 6 B2
Milborne Port 6 B4
Milborne St. Andrew 6 C5
Mildenhall 15 E1
Mile End 15 F3
Milfield 33 G4
Milford 8 A3
Milford Haven
  (Aberdaugleddau)
  10 B4
Milford on Sea 7 E5
Millbrook 4 C6
Millhouse 31 E3
Millom 27 G6
Millport 31 F4
Milltown of
  Rothiemay 41 E3
Milnathort 36 D4
Milngavie 31 H3
Milnrow 23 F4
Milnthorpe 27 H6
Milovaig 38 A3
Milton (Strathconon)
  High 39 D3
Milton (Drumnadrochit)
  High 39 D4
Milton *P&K* 36 C2
Milton Keynes 13 H3
Milton of Campsie 31 H3
Milverton 5 G2
Minard 31 F2
Minchinhampton 12 C4
Minehead 5 F1
Minera 17 F3
Minnigaff 26 C2
Minster (Sheppey)
  Kent 15 F6
Minster (Thanet)
  Kent 15 H6
Minsterley 17 G5
Mintlaw 41 G3
Mirfield 24 A3
Misterton 24 D5
Mitcheldean 12 B4
Mobberley 23 E6
Modbury 4 D6
Moelfre 16 C1
Moffat 32 B5
Mold
  (Yr Wyddgrug) 22 B6
Molescroft 25 E2
Moniaive 27 E1
Monifieth 37 E3
Monimail 36 D4

Monkokehampton 4 D3
Monks Eleigh 15 F2
Monmouth
  (Trefynwy) 12 B4
Monreith 26 C3
Montgomery 17 F6
Montrose 37 G2
Moorends 24 C4
Morar 38 C6
Morebattle 33 F4
Morecambe 22 C1
Morenish 36 A3
Moresby Parks 27 F4
Moreton 22 B5
Moretonhampstead 5 E4
Moreton-in-Marsh 13 E3
Morfa Nefyn 16 A3
Morley 24 A3
Morpeth 28 D1
Morriston 11 E5
Mortehoe 4 C1
Mortimer's Cross 12 A1
Morton (Bourne)
  Lincs 20 A3
Morton (Gainsborough)
  Lincs 24 D5
Morville 18 A5
Mosborough 24 B5
Moscow 31 G4
Mossat 40 D5
Mossbank 45 H3
Mossblown 31 G5
Mossley 23 F4
Mosstodloch 40 D2
Motherwell 32 A3
Moulsecoomb 8 C5
Moulton *Lincs* 20 B3
Moulton *Suff* 14 D1
Mountain Ash 11 G5
Mountbenger 32 D4
Mountsorrel 19 F4
Moy 40 A4
Much Wenlock 18 A4
Muchalls 41 F6
Muir of Fowlis 41 E5
Muir of Ord 39 H3
Muirdrum 37 F3
Muirhead 37 E3
Muirkirk 31 H5
Mulbarton 21 F4
Mulben 40 D3
Mullion 3 F6
Mundesley 21 G3
Mundford 20 D5
Munlochy 39 H3
Murton 29 E3
Musbury 5 G4
Musselburgh 32 D2
Muthill 36 B4
Mybster 43 G3
Mytholmroyd 23 F3

N

Nailsea 12 A6
Nailsworth 12 C5
Nairn 40 A3
Nantwich 18 A2
Nantyglo 11 H4
Narberth 10 C4
Narborough *Leics* 19 F5
Narborough *Norf* 20 D4
Nateby 28 B5
Nazeing 14 C4
Near Sawrey 27 H6
Neath
  (Castell-nedd) 11 F5
Necton 20 D4
Needham Market 15 F2
Needingworth 14 C1
Nefyn 16 B3
Neilston 31 G4
Nelson 23 E3

Nenthead 28 B3
Neston 22 B6
Nether Langwith 24 C6
Nether Stowey 5 G2
Netherley 41 F6
Netherton 33 G5
Nethy Bridge 40 B4
Nettlebed 13 H5
Nettleham 25 E6
New Abbey 27 F2
New Aberdour 41 F2
New Addington 14 C6
New Alresford 7 G3
New Ash Green 14 D6
New Byth 41 F3
New Cumnock 31 H6
New Deer 41 F3
New Galloway 26 D2
New Leeds 41 G3
New Luce 26 B2
New Mills 23 F5
New Milton 7 E5
New Mistley 15 G3
New Pitsligo 41 F3
New Quay 10 D2
New Radnor 11 H1
New Romney 9 F4
New Rossington 24 C5
New Tredegar 11 H4
Newark-on-Trent 19 G2
Newbiggin-by-the-
  Sea 29 E1
Newbigging 32 B3
Newbold Verdon 19 E4
Newborough 20 A4
Newbridge 11 H5
Newburgh *Aber* 41 G4
Newburgh *Fife* 36 D4
Newburn 28 D2
Newbury 13 F6
Newby Bridge 27 H6
Newcastle 17 F6
Newcastle Emlyn 10 D2
Newcastle upon
  Tyne 28 D2
Newcastleton 27 H1
Newcastle-under-
  Lyme 18 B2
Newent 12 C3
Newhaven 8 C5
Newick 8 C4
Newington 15 E6
Newlyn 3 E5
Newmachar 41 F5
Newmains 32 A3
Newmarket 14 D1
Newmill 40 D3
Newmilns 31 H5
Newnham 12 B4
Newport *Essex* 14 D3
Newport *High* 43 G4
Newport *IoW* 7 G5
Newport (Casnewydd)
  Newport 12 A5
Newport *Pembs* 10 B3
Newport *Tel&W* 18 B4
Newport Pagnell 13 H2
Newport-on-Tay 37 E3
Newquay 3 G3
Newton *A&B* 31 E2
Newton *Lancs* 22 D2
Newton Abbot 5 E4
Newton Aycliffe 28 D4
Newton Ferrers 4 D6
Newton Mearns 31 H4
Newton Poppleford 5 F4
Newton St. Cyres 5 E4
Newton Stewart 26 C2
Newtonhill 41 G6
Newton-le-
  Willows 22 D5
Newtonmore 40 A6
Newtown *Here* 12 B2

Newtown (Y Drenewydd)
  Powys 17 F6
Newtown
  St. Boswells 33 E4
Newtyle 36 D2
Neyland 10 B4
Ninemile Bar
  (Crocketford) 27 E2
Ninfield 9 E5
Nisbet 33 E4
Norham 33 G3
Normanton 24 B3
North Baddesley 7 F3
North Ballachulish 35 F1
North Berwick 33 E1
North Cave 24 D3
North Cheriton 6 B3
North Cowton 28 D5
North Duffield 24 C3
North Elmham 21 E3
North Ferriby 25 E3
North Grimston 24 D1
North Hykeham 25 E6
North Kessock 39 H3
North Leigh 13 F4
North Middleton 32 D3
North Molton 5 E2
North Queensferry 32 C1
North Roe 45 H2
North Shields 29 E2
North Somercotes 25 G5
North Sunderland 33 H4
North Thoresby 25 F5
North Walsham 21 F3
North Weald
  Bassett 14 C4
North Wingfield 24 B6
Northallerton 29 E6
Northam 4 C2
Northampton 13 H1
Northfleet 14 D6
Northill 14 B2
Northleach 13 E4
Northton 44 C5
Northwich 22 D6
Northwood 7 F5
Norton *NYorks* 24 D1
Norton *Suff* 15 F1
Norton Canes 18 C4
Norton Fitzwarren 5 G2
Norwich 21 F4
Nottingham 19 F2
Nuneaton 19 E5

O

Oadby 19 F4
Oakdale 11 H5
Oakengates 18 A4
Oakham 19 G4
Oakley *Bucks* 13 G4
Oakley *Fife* 32 B1
Oakley *Hants* 7 H2
Oban (An t-Òban) 35 E3
Ochiltree 31 H5
Ockbrook 19 E3
Ockle 34 D1
Oddsta 45 J2
Odiham 7 H2
Ogmore 11 F6
Ogmore Vale 11 G5
Okehampton 4 D4
Old Clipstone 24 C6
Old Colwyn 16 D2
Old Dailly 26 B1
Old Felixstowe 15 H3
Old Leake 20 B2
Old Town 28 A6
Oldbury 18 C5
Oldham 23 F4
Oldland 12 B6
Oldmeldrum 41 F4
Olgrinmore 43 F3

Ollaberry 45 H2
Ollerton 24 C6
Olney 13 H2
Olveston 12 B5
Ombersley 12 C1
Onchan 26 C6
Onich 35 F1
Orford 15 H2
Ormesby
  St. Margaret 21 G4
Ormiston 32 D2
Ormskirk 22 C4
Orphir 45 C3
Orpington 14 C6
Orrell 22 D4
Orton 28 A5
Orton Longueville 20 A5
Oskaig 38 C4
Ossett 24 A3
Oswaldkirk 24 C1
Oswaldtwistle 23 E3
Oswestry 17 F4
Otford 8 D3
Otley *Suff* 15 G2
Otley *WYorks* 24 A2
Otter Ferry 31 E2
Otterburn 28 B1
Ottery St. Mary 5 F4
Oughtibridge 24 B5
Oulton 21 H5
Oundle 19 H5
Outwell 20 C4
Over Wallop 7 E3
Overbister 45 D1
Overseal 18 D4
Overton *Hants* 7 G2
Overton *Wrex* 17 G3
Overtown 32 A3
Oxenhope 23 F3
Oxford 13 G4
Oxnam 33 E5
Oxshott 14 B6
Oxted 8 C3
Oxton 32 D3
Oykel Bridge 42 C5

P

Padbury 13 H3
Paddock Wood 8 D3
Padiham 23 E3
Padstow 3 H3
Paignton 5 E5
Painswick 12 C4
Paisley 31 G3
Palnackie 27 E3
Pandy 12 A3
Pangbourne 13 G6
Pant-y-dwr 11 G1
Papworth Everard 14 B1
Par 3 H4
Parbold 22 C4
Parkgate 27 F1
Partington 23 E5
Partney 25 G6
Parton 27 F4
Patchway 12 B5
Pateley Bridge 24 A1
Path of Condie 36 C4
Patna 31 G5
Patrick 26 B5
Patrington 25 G3
Patterdale 27 H5
Paulton 6 B2
Paxton 33 G3
Peacehaven 8 C5
Peasedown St. John 6 C2
Peebles 32 C3
Peel 26 B5
Pegswood 28 D1
Peinchorran 38 C4
Pelsall 18 C4
Pelynt 4 B6

Pembrey **10** D4
Pembridge **12** A2
Pembroke **10** B4
Pembroke Dock
  (Doc Penfro) **10** B4
Pembury **8** D3
Penally **10** C5
Penarth **11** H6
Pencader **10** D3
Pencaitland **32** D2
Pencoed **11** G5
Pendeen **3** E5
Pendine **10** C4
Pendlebury **23** E4
Penicuik **32** C2
Peninver **30** D5
Penistone **24** A4
Penkridge **18** C4
Penley **17** G4
Penmaenmawr **16** D2
Pennyghael **34** D3
Penpont **27** E1
Penrhiw-pal **10** D2
Penrhyn Bay **16** D1
Penrhyndeudraeth **16** C4
Penrith **28** A4
Penruddock **28** A4
Pensarn **3** G5
Pensilva **4** B5
Pentir **16** C2
Pentraeth **16** C2
Pentre **11** G5
Pentrefoelas **16** D3
Penwortham **22** D3
Penybont **11** H1
Pen-y-bont-fawr **17** E4
Penygraig **11** G5
Penygroes **16** B3
Penywaun **11** G4
Penzance **3** E5
Perranporth **3** G4
Pershore **12** D2
Perth (Peairt) **36** D3
Peterborough **20** A5
Peterculter **41** F5
Peterhead **41** H3
Peterlee **29** E3
Petersfield **7** H3
Petworth **8** A4
Pevensey **8** D5
Pewsey **13** E6
Pickering **29** G6
Piddletrenthide **6** C5
Pierowall **45** C1
Pilgrims Hatch **14** D5
Pilling **22** C2
Pilning **12** B5
Pimperne **6** D4
Pinchbeck **20** A3
Pinhoe **5** F4
Pinwherry **26** B1
Pirbright **8** A3
Pirnmill **30** D4
Pitagowan **36** B1
Pitlochry **36** C2
Pitmedden **41** F4
Pitscottie **37** E4
Pitt **7** F3
Pittentrail **43** E5
Pittenweem **37** F4
Plean **32** A1
Pleasley **24** C6
Plumb **10** D2
Plymouth **4** C6
Plympton **4** D6
Plymstock **4** D6
Pocklington **24** D2
Polbeth **32** B2
Polegate **8** D5
Polesworth **18** D4
Polloch **35** E1
Polmont **32** B2
Polperro **4** B6
Polwarth **33** F3

Pondersbridge **20** A5
Pontardawe **11** F4
Pontarddulais **11** E4
Pontefract **24** B3
Ponteland **28** D2
Pontesbury **17** G5
Pontllanfraith **11** H5
Pontrhydfendigaid **11** F1
Pontrilas **12** A3
Pontyberem **11** E4
Pontycymer **11** G5
Pontypool **11** H4
Pontypridd **11** G5
Pool **24** A2
Poole **6** D5
Poolewe **38** D1
Pooley Bridge **27** H4
Porlock **5** E1
Port Appin **35** F2
Port Askaig **30** B3
Port Bannatyne **31** E3
Port Driseach **31** E3
Port Ellen **30** B4
Port Erin **26** B6
Port Eynon **10** D5
Port Glasgow **31** G3
Port Henderson **38** C2
Port Logan **26** A3
Port nan Long **44** B6
Port of Menteith **31** H1
Port of Ness **44** F1
Port St. Mary **26** B6
Porth **11** G5
Porthcawl **11** F6
Porthleven **3** F5
Porthmadog **16** C4
Portishead **12** A6
Portknockie **40** D2
Portlethen **41** G6
Portmahomack **40** B1
Portnacon **42** C2
Portnacroish **35** F2
Portnaguran **44** F3
Portnahaven **30** A4
Portnalong **38** B2
Portpatrick **26** A3
Portreath **3** F4
Portree **38** B3
Portsmouth **7** G5
Portsoy **41** E2
Potterne **6** D2
Potters Bar **14** B4
Potton **14** B2
Poulton-le-Fylde **22** C3
Powburn **33** G5
Powick **12** C2
Powmill **32** B1
Poynton **23** F5
Prees **18** A3
Preesall **22** C2
Prescot **22** C5
Prestatyn **22** A5
Prestbury *ChesE* **23** E6
Prestbury *Glos* **12** D3
Presteigne **12** A1
Preston *Dorset* **6** C5
Preston *ERid* **25** F3
Preston *Lancs* **22** D3
Preston *ScBord* **33** F3
Prestonpans **32** D2
Prestwich **23** E4
Prestwick **31** G5
Prestwood **13** H4
Princes Risborough **13** H4
Princethorpe **13** F1
Princetown **4** D5
Probus **3** G4
Prudhoe **28** D2

Puddletown **6** C5
Pudsey **24** A3
Pulborough **8** A5
Pumsaint **11** E2
Purfleet **14** D6
Puriton **6** A2
Purley **14** C6
Purley on Thames **13** G6
Purton **12** D5
Pwllheli **16** B4
Pyle **11** F5

Q

Quarff **45** H5
Quedgeley **12** C4
Queenborough **15** F6
Queensbury **24** A3
Queensferry
  (South Queensferry)
  Edin **32** C2
Queensferry
  Flints **22** C6
Queniborough **19** F4
Quernmore **22** D1

R

Rackheath **21** F4
Radcliffe **23** E4
Radcliffe on Trent **19** F3
Radford Semele **13** F1
Radlett **14** B4
Radstock **6** B2
Rafford **40** B3
Raglan **12** A4
Rainford **22** C4
Rainhill **22** C5
Rainow **23** F6
Rainworth **19** F2
Rait **36** D3
Rampside **22** B1
Ramsbottom **23** E4
Ramsbury **13** E6
Ramsey *Cambs* **20** A5
Ramsey *IoM* **26** C5
Ramsey St. Mary's **20** A5
Ramsgate **15** H6
Ranskill **24** C5
Rathillet **37** E3
Ratho **32** C2
Rattray **36** D2
Raunds **14** A1
Ravenglass **27** F6
Ravenshead **19** F2
Rawcliffe *ERid* **24** C3
Rawcliffe *York* **24** C2
Rawmarsh **24** B5
Rawtenstall **23** E3
Rayleigh **15** E5
Rayne **15** E4
Reading **13** H6
Reay **43** F2
Red Point **38** D2
Red Roses **10** C4
Redbourn **14** B4
Redcar **29** F4
Redcastle **39** H3
Redcliff Bay **12** A6
Redditch **12** D1
Redford **37** F2
Redhill **8** B3
Redlynch **7** E4
Redruth **3** G4
Reepham **21** E3
Reiff **42** A5
Reigate **8** B3
Reiss **43** H1
Renfrew **31** H3
Rennington **33** H5
Repton **19** E3
Rescobie **37** F2
Resolven **11** F4

Reston **33** F2
Retford
  (East Retford) **24** D5
Reydon **15** H1
Rhayader
  (Rhaeadr Gwy) **11** G1
Rhiconich **42** B3
Rhoose **11** G6
Rhos **11** H4
Rhosllanerchrugog **17** F3
Rhôs-on-Sea **16** D1
Rhossili **10** D5
Rhu **31** F2
Rhuddlan **22** A6
Rhyl **22** A5
Rhymney **11** H4
Rhynie **40** D4
Ribchester **22** D3
Richmond *GtLon* **14** B6
Richmond *NYorks* **28** D5
Rickarton **41** F6
Rickinghall **15** F1
Rickmansworth **14** A5
Riding Mill **28** C2
Rigside **32** A4
Ringford **26** D3
Ringmer **8** C5
Ringwood **7** E4
Ripley *Derbys* **19** E2
Ripley *NYorks* **24** A1
Ripon **24** B1
Ripple **12** C3
Ripponden **23** F4
Risca **11** H5
Rishton **23** E3
Risley **19** E3
Roade **13** H2
Roadside **43** G2
Roadside of
  Kinneff **37** G1
Roath **11** H6
Roberton *ScBord* **32** D5
Roberton *SLan* **32** B4
Robin Hood's Bay **29** H5
Rocester **18** D3
Rochdale **23** E4
Roche **3** H4
Rochester *Med* **15** E6
Rochester *N'umb* **28** B1
Rochford **15** E5
Rock **12** C1
Rockcliffe **27** E3
Rockingham **19** G5
Rode Heath **18** B2
Rodel **44** C5
Rodney Stoke **6** A2
Rogart **43** E5
Rogate **7** H3
Rogerstone **11** H5
Romannobridge **32** C3
Romford **14** D5
Romsey **7** F3
Romsley **18** C5
Ropley **7** G3
Ropsley **19** H3
Rosedale Abbey **29** G6
Rosehearty **41** G2
Rosemarkie **40** A3
Rosewell **32** C2
Roshven **35** E1
Roskhill **38** A3
Roslin **32** C2
Rossett **17** G3
Rossington **24** C5
Ross-on-Wye **12** B3
Rothbury **33** G5
Rotherfield **8** D4
Rotherham **24** B5
Rothes **40** C3
Rothesay **31** E3
Rothley **19** F4
Rothwell *N'hants* **19** G5
Rothwell *WYorks* **24** B3

Rottingdean **8** C5
Roughton **21** F3
Roundway **12** D6
Rowde **12** D6
Rowlands Gill **28** D3
Roxton **14** B2
Royal Leamington
  Spa **13** F1
Royal Tunbridge
  Wells **8** D4
Roybridge **39** F6
Roydon **21** E5
Royston *Herts* **14** C2
Royston *SYorks* **24** B4
Royton **23** F4
Ruabon **17** G3
Ruardean **12** B4
Ruddington **19** F3
Rudgwick **8** A4
Rudston **25** E1
Rufford **22** C5
Rugby **13** G1
Rugeley **18** C4
Rumney **11** H6
Runcorn **22** D5
Runwell **15** E5
Rushall **18** C4
Rushden **14** A1
Rushmere
  St. Andrew **15** G2
Ruskington **19** H2
Ruspidge **12** B4
Rustington **8** A5
Rutherglen **31** H3
Ruthin (Rhuthun) **17** F3
Ruyton-XI-Towns **17** G4
Ryde **9** F4
Rye **9** F4
Ryhall **19** H4

S

Sacriston **28** D3
Saddell **30** D5
Saffron Walden **14** D3
Saham Toney **20** D4
Saighdinis **44** B6
St. Abbs **33** G2
St. Agnes **3** G4
St. Albans **14** B4
St. Andrews **37** F4
St. Anne **5** H5
St. Asaph **22** A6
St. Athan **11** G6
St. Austell **3** H4
St. Bees **27** F5
St. Brelade **5** G6
St. Briavels **12** B4
St. Brides Major **11** F6
St. Buryan **3** E5
St. Clears (Sanclêr) **10** C4
St. Columb Major **3** H3
St. Combs **41** H2
St. Cyrus **37** G1
St. David's **10** A3
St. Day **3** G4
St. Dennis **3** H4
St. Dogmaels **10** C2
St. Endellion **3** H3
St. Enoder **3** G4
St. Fergus **41** H3
St. Fillans **36** A3
St. Germans **4** C6
St. Helens **22** D5
St. Helier **5** H6
St. Ishmael **10** D4
St. Ive **4** C5
St. Ives *Cambs* **14** C1
St. Ives *Corn* **3** F4
St. John **5** H6
St. John's Chapel **28** B4
St. John's Town of
  Dalry **26** D1

St. Just 3 E5
St. Just in Roseland 3 G5
St. Keverne 3 G6
St. Leonards 7 E4
St. Margaret's at
  Cliffe 9 H3
St. Margaret's
  Hope 45 C4
St. Martin 5 H5
St. Martin's 17 G4
St. Mary Bourne 7 F2
St. Mary's 45 C3
St. Mary's Bay 9 F4
St. Mawes 3 G5
St. Merryn 3 G3
St. Monans 37 F4
St. Neots 14 B2
St. Osyth 15 G4
St. Peter Port 5 H5
St. Peter's 15 H6
St. Sampson 5 H5
St. Stephen 3 H4
St. Teath 3 H2
Salcombe 5 E7
Sale 23 E5
Salen A&B 34 D2
Salen High 34 D1
Salford 23 E5
Salfords 8 B3
Salhouse 21 G4
Saline 32 B1
Salisbury 7 E3
Salsburgh 32 A2
Saltash 4 C6
Saltburn-by-the-
  Sea 29 F4
Saltcoats 31 F4
Saltdean 8 C5
Saltford 12 B6
Saltney 22 C6
Sanaigmore 30 A3
Sandbach 23 E6
Sandgarth 45 D3
Sandhead 26 A3
Sandhurst 13 H6
Sandiacre 19 E3
Sandness 45 G4
Sandown 7 G5
Sandplace 4 B6
Sandridge 14 B4
Sandsend 29 G5
Sandwich 9 H3
Sandwick 45 H5
Sandy 14 B2
Sandygate 26 C5
Sanquhar 32 A5
Sapcote 19 E5
Sarre 15 G6
Satley 28 D3
Saundersfoot 10 C4
Sawbridgeworth 14 C4
Sawston 14 C2
Sawtry 20 A5
Saxilby 24 D6
Saxmundham 15 H1
Saxthorpe 21 F3
Scalasaig 30 B2
Scalby 29 H6
Scalloway 45 H5
Scampton 25 E6
Scarborough 29 H6
Scarcliffe 24 B6
Scardroy 39 F3
Scarinish 34 A2
Scarisbrick 22 C4
Scleddau 10 B3
Scole 15 G1
Scone 36 D3
Sconser 38 C4
Scorton 28 D6
Scotch Corner 28 D5
Scotter 24 D4
Scotton 28 D6

Scourie 42 B3
Scousburgh 45 H6
Scrabster 43 F2
Scraptoft 19 F4
Scremerston 33 G3
Scunthorpe 24 D4
Seaford 8 C6
Seaham 29 E3
Seahouses 33 H4
Seamer 29 H6
Seamill 31 F4
Seascale 27 F5
Seaton Cumb 27 F4
Seaton Devon 5 G4
Seaton Delaval 29 E2
Seaton Sluice 29 E2
Sedbergh 28 A6
Sedgebrook 19 G3
Sedgefield 29 E4
Sedgley 18 C3
Seend 12 D6
Seghill 28 D2
Seighford 18 B3
Selattyn 17 F4
Selby 24 C3
Selkirk 32 D4
Sellafield 27 F5
Sellindge 9 F4
Selsey 7 H5
Selston 19 E2
Send 8 A3
Sennen 3 E5
Sennybridge 11 G3
Settle 23 E1
Seven Sisters 11 F4
Sevenoaks 8 D3
Severn Beach 12 B5
Sgiogarstaigh 44 F1
Shaftesbury 6 C3
Shalfleet 7 F5
Shalford 8 A3
Shanklin 7 G5
Shap 28 A5
Sharpness 12 B4
Shavington 18 A2
Shaw 23 F4
Shawbost 44 D2
Sheering 14 D4
Sheerness 15 F6
Sheffield 24 B5
Shefford 14 B3
Shelf 24 A3
Shenstone 18 D4
Shepley 24 A4
Shepperton 14 A6
Shepshed 19 E4
Shepton Mallet 6 B2
Sherborne 6 B4
Sherborne St. John 7 G2
Sherburn 29 E3
Sherburn in Elmet 24 B3
Shere 8 A3
Sheriff Hutton 24 C1
Sheriffhales 18 B4
Sheringham 21 F2
Sherston 12 C5
Shevington 22 D4
Shiel Bridge 39 E5
Shieldaig 38 D3
Shifnal 18 B4
Shilbottle 33 H5
Shildon 28 D4
Shinfield 13 H6
Shinness Lodge 42 D5
Shiplake 13 H6
Shipley 24 A3
Shipston on Stour 13 E2
Shipton NYorks 24 C2
Shipton Shrop 18 A5
Shipton-under-
  Wychwood 13 E4
Shirebrook 24 C6
Shiremoor 29 E2

Shirenewton 12 A5
Shirland 19 E2
Shoeburyness 15 F5
Shoreham 14 D6
Shoreham-by-Sea 8 B5
Shotley Gate 15 G3
Shotton 22 C6
Shotts 32 A2
Shrewsbury 17 F5
Shrewton 6 D2
Shrivenham 13 E5
Sible Hedingham 15 E3
Sibsey 20 B2
Sidbury 5 G4
Sidcup 14 C6
Sidford 5 G4
Sidley 9 E5
Sidmouth 5 G4
Sigglesthorne 25 F2
Sileby 19 F4
Silloth 27 G3
Silsden 23 F2
Silverdale 22 C1
Silverstone 13 G2
Silverton 5 F3
Simonsbath 5 E2
Sittingbourne 15 F6
Skaill 45 B3
Skegness 25 G6
Skeld 45 H4
Skelmersdale 22 C4
Skelmorlie 31 F3
Skelton 29 F5
Skelwick 45 C1
Skenfrith 12 A3
Skerray 42 D2
Skipness 31 E4
Skipsea 25 F2
Skipton 23 F2
Skirlaugh 25 F3
Slaidburn 23 E2
Slaithwaite 23 F4
Slamannan 32 A2
Sleaford 19 H2
Sledmere 25 E1
Sleights 29 G5
Sligachan 38 B4
Slinfold 8 B4
Slough 14 A6
Smailholm 33 E4
Smalley 19 E2
Smeeth 9 F4
Smethwick 18 C5
Snainton 29 H6
Snaith 24 C3
Snettisham 20 C3
Snitterfield 13 E2
Snodland 15 E6
Soham 14 D1
Solihull 13 E1
Sollas 44 B6
Solva 10 A3
Somercotes 19 E2
Somersham 14 C1
Somerton 6 A3
Sompting 8 B5
Sonning Common 13 H5
Sorbie 26 C3
Sorisdale 34 B1
Sorn 31 H5
South Anston 24 C5
South Bank 29 F4
South Benfleet 15 E5
South Brent 4 D5
South Cave 25 E3
South Chard 6 A4
South Harting 7 H4
South Hetton 29 E3
South Kelsey 25 E5
South Kirkby 24 B4
South Leverton 24 D5
South Lopham 21 E5
South Molton 5 E2

South Normanton 19 E2
South Ockendon 14 D5
South Oxhey 14 B5
South Petherton 6 A4
South Queensferry
  (Queensferry) 32 C2
South Shields 29 E2
South Woodham
  Ferrers 15 E5
South Wootton 20 C3
Southam 13 F1
Southampton 7 F4
Southborough 8 D3
Southbourne 7 H4
Southdean 33 E5
Southend 30 C6
Southend-on-Sea 15 E5
Southery 20 C5
Southgate 14 B5
Southminster 15 F5
Southport 22 C4
Southwell 19 G2
Southwick 6 C2
Southwold 21 H6
Sowerby 29 E6
Sowerby Bridge 23 F3
Spalding 20 A3
Spean Bridge 39 F6
Speen 13 F6
Spennymoor 28 D4
Spey Bay 40 D2
Spilsby 25 G6
Spinningdale 39 H1
Spittal 45 H3
Spittal of Glenshee 36 D1
Spixworth 21 F4
Spofforth 24 B2
Springholm 27 E2
Springside 31 G5
Sproatley 25 F3
Sprowston 21 F4
Sproxton 29 F6
Stadhampton 13 G5
Staffin 38 B2
Stafford 18 C3
Staindrop 28 D4
Staines 14 A6
Stainforth NYorks 23 E1
Stainforth SYorks 24 C4
Staintondale 29 H6
Stalbridge 6 C4
Stalham 21 G3
Stalling Busk 28 C6
Stalybridge 23 F5
Stamford 19 H4
Stamfordham 28 C2
Standish 22 D4
Standon 14 C3
Stane 32 A3
Stanford-le-Hope 14 D5
Stanhoe 20 D3
Stanhope 28 C4
Stanley Dur 28 D3
Stanley P&K 36 D3
Stanley WYorks 24 B3
Stannington 28 D2
Stansted
  Mountfitchet 14 D3
Stanton 15 F1
Stanway 15 F3
Stapleford 19 E3
Staplehurst 9 E3
Starcross 5 F4
Startforth 28 C5
Staunton 12 C3
Staveley 24 B6
Staxton 25 E1
Steeple Claydon 13 G3
Steeton 23 F2
Stenhousemuir 32 A1
Stenton 33 E2
Stevenage 14 B3
Stevenston 31 F4

Stewarton 31 G4
Steyning 8 B5
Stibb Cross 4 C3
Stichill 33 F4
Stickney 20 B2
Stilligarry 44 B8
Stillington 24 C1
Stilton 20 A5
Stirling 32 A1
Stobo 32 C4
Stock 14 D5
Stockbridge 7 F3
Stockport 23 E5
Stocksbridge 24 A5
Stocksfield 28 C2
Stockton Heath 22 D5
Stockton-on-Tees 29 E4
Stoer 42 A4
Stoke Albany 19 G5
Stoke Ash 15 G1
Stoke Holy Cross 21 F4
Stoke Mandeville 13 H4
Stoke Poges 14 A5
Stoke Prior 12 D1
Stoke-by-Nayland 15 F3
Stokenchurch 13 H5
Stokenham 5 E6
Stoke-on-Trent 18 B2
Stokesay 17 G6
Stokesley 29 F5
Stone Glos 12 B5
Stone Staffs 18 B3
Stonehaven 41 F6
Stonehouse Glos 12 C4
Stonehouse SLan 32 A3
Stoneykirk 26 A3
Stony Stratford 13 H2
Stonybeck 45 F6
Stornoway
  (Steornabhagh) 44 E3
Storrington 8 A5
Stotfold 14 B3
Stourbridge 18 B5
Stourport-on-
  Severn 12 C1
Stow 32 D3
Stowmarket 15 F2
Stow-on-the-Wold 13 E3
Strachan 41 E6
Strachur 31 F1
Stradbroke 15 G1
Stradishall 15 E2
Stradsett 20 C4
Straloch 36 C1
Stranraer 26 A2
Stratford-upon-
  Avon 13 E2
Strathaven 32 A3
Strathblane 31 H3
Strathdon 40 D5
Strathmiglo 36 D4
Strathpeffer 39 G3
Strathy 43 E2
Strathyre 31 H1
Stratton 4 B3
Stratton
  St. Margaret 13 E5
Streatley 13 G5
Street 6 A3
Strensall 24 C1
Stretford 23 E5
Stretham 14 D1
Stretton 18 D3
Strichen 41 F4
Stromeferry 38 D4
Stromness 45 B3
Stronachlachar 31 G1
Strone 31 F2
Strontian 35 E1
Stroud 12 C4
Stuartfield 41 G3
Studley 12 D1
Sturminster Newton 6 C4

Sturry **15** G6
Sturton le Steeple **24** D5
Sudbury *Derbys* **18** D3
Sudbury *Suff* **15** E2
Sully **11** H6
Sumburgh **45** H6
Summer Bridge **24** A1
Sunbury **14** B6
Sunderland **29** E3
Sunninghill **14** A6
Surfleet **20** A3
Sutterton **20** A3
Sutton *Cambs* **14** C1
Sutton *GtLon* **14** B6
Sutton Bridge **20** B3
Sutton Coldfield **18** D5
Sutton Courtenay **13** F5
Sutton in Ashfield **19** E2
Sutton on Trent **24** D6
Sutton Valence **9** E3
Sutton-on-the-
   Forest **24** C1
Swadlincote **19** E4
Swaffham **20** D4
Swanage **6** D6
Swanland **25** E3
Swanley **14** D6
Swanscombe **14** D6
Swansea
   (Abertawe) **11** E5
Swanton Morley **21** E4
Sway **7** E5
Swindon **13** E5
Swindon Village **12** D3
Swinefleet **24** D3
Swinton *GtMan* **23** E4
Swinton *ScBord* **33** F3
Swinton *SYorks* **24** B5
Symbister **45** J3
Symington *SAyr* **31** G5
Symington *SLan* **32** B4
Synod Inn **10** D2
Syre **42** D3
Syston **19** F4

T

Tadcaster **24** B2
Tadley **13** G6
Taffs Well **11** H5
Tain **40** A1
Takeley **14** D3
Talgarreg **10** D2
Talgarth **11** H3
Taliesin **16** C6
Talisker **38** B4
Talladale **39** E2
Talmine **42** D2
Tamworth **18** D4
Tannadice **37** E2
Tansley **19** E2
Tarbert (Kintyre)
   A&B **30** D3
Tarbert (Jura)
   A&B **30** C2
Tarbert (An Tairbeart)
   WIsles **44** D4
Tarbet **31** G1
Tarbolton **31** G5
Tarfside **40** D6
Tarleton **22** C3
Tarporley **22** D6
Tarrel **40** A1
Tarves **41** F4
Tarvin **22** D6
Tattershall **20** A2
Taunton **5** G2
Taverham **21** F4
Tavistock **4** C5
Tayinloan **30** C4
Taynuilt **35** F2
Tayport **37** E3
Tayvallich **30** D2

Tealing **37** E3
Teangue **38** C5
Tebay **28** A5
Teignmouth **5** F5
Telford **18** A4
Temple Bar **11** E2
Temple Sowerby **28** A4
Templeton **10** C4
Tenbury Wells **12** B1
Tenby (Dinbych-y-
   pysgod) **10** C4
Tenterden **9** E4
Terrington **24** C1
Terrington
   St. Clement **20** C3
Tetbury **12** C5
Tetford **25** G6
Tetney **25** G4
Teviothead **32** D5
Tewkesbury **12** C3
Teynham **15** F6
Thame **13** H4
Thatcham **13** G6
Thaxted **14** D3
The Mumbles **11** E5
The Stocks **9** F4
Theale **13** G6
Thetford **20** D5
Thirsk **29** E6
Thornaby-on-Tees **29** E5
Thornbury **12** B5
Thorne **24** C4
Thorney **20** A4
Thorngumbald **25** F3
Thornhill *D&G* **27** E1
Thornhill *Stir* **31** H1
Thornley **29** E4
Thornton *Fife* **32** C2
Thornton *Lancs* **22** C2
Thornton *Mersey* **22** C4
Thornton-le-Dale **29** G6
Thorpe Market **21** F3
Thorpe on the Hill **25** E6
Thorpe St. Andrew **21** F4
Thorpe-le-Soken **15** G3
Thorpeness **15** H2
Thrapston **14** A1
Threlkeld **27** H4
Threshfield **23** F1
Thropton **33** G5
Thrumster **43** H3
Thrupp **12** D3
Thrybergh **24** B5
Thundersley **15** E5
Thurcroft **24** C5
Thurlby **20** A4
Thurmaston **19** F4
Thurnscoe **24** B4
Thursby **27** H3
Thurso
   (Inbhir Theòrsa) **43** G2
Thurton **21** G4
Thwaite **28** B6
Tibbermore **36** C3
Tibshelf **24** A6
Ticehurst **8** D4
Tickhill **24** C5
Ticknall **19** E3
Tidenham **12** B5
Tideswell **24** A6
Tidworth **7** E2
Tighnabruaich **31** E3
Tilbury **14** D6
Tilehurst **13** G6
Tillicoultry **32** B1
Tillyfourie **41** E5
Tilston **17** G3
Timsbury **6** B2
Timsgearraidh **44** C3
Tingewick **13** G3
Tingwall **45** C2
Tintagel **3** H2
Tintern Parva **12** B4

Tiptree **15** E4
Tisbury **6** D3
Tiverton **5** F3
Toab **45** H6
Tobermory **34** D2
Toberonochy **30** D1
Toddington
   CenBeds **14** A3
Toddington *Glos* **12** D3
Todmorden **23** F3
Togston **33** H5
Tolastadh Úr **44** F2
Toll of Birness **41** G4
Tollesbury **15** F4
Tolleshunt D'Arcy **15** F4
Tomatin **40** A4
Tomich **39** H2
Tomintoul **40** C5
Tomnavoulin **40** C4
Tonbridge **8** D3
Tongland **27** E3
Tongue **42** D3
Tonyrefail **11** G5
Topcliffe **24** B1
Topsham **5** F4
Tore **39** H3
Tormore **31** E5
Torphichen **32** B2
Torphins **41** E5
Torpoint **4** C6
Torquay **5** E5
Torrance **31** H3
Torridon **39** E3
Torrin **38** C4
Torthorwald **27** F2
Torver **27** G6
Toscaig **38** D4
Tosside **23** E2
Totland **7** F5
Totnes **5** E5
Tottington **23** E4
Totton **7** F4
Tow Law **28** D4
Towcester **13** G2
Town Yetholm **33** F4
Townhead of
   Greenlaw **27** E2
Towyn **22** A6
Tranent **32** D2
Trawsfynydd **16** D3
Trecastle **11** F3
Tredegar **11** H4
Tredington **13** E2
Treeton **24** B5
Trefeglwys **17** F5
Trefriw **16** D2
Tregaron **11** E2
Tregony **3** H4
Tregynon **17** E6
Treharris **11** G5
Treherbert **11** G5
Trelech **10** C3
Trelleck **12** B4
Tremadog **16** C3
Trenance **3** G3
Treorchy **11** G5
Tressait **36** B1
Tretower **11** H3
Trimdon **29** E4
Trimsaran **10** D4
Tring **14** A4
Trinity **37** F1
Trochry **36** C2
Troedyrhiw **11** G4
Troon **31** G5
Troutbeck **27** H5
Troutbeck Bridge **27** H5
Trowbridge **6** C2
Trumpington **14** C2
Truro **3** G4
Tudweiliog **16** A4
Tummel Bridge **36** B2

Tunbridge Wells **8** D4
Tunstall **15** H2
Turnberry **31** F6
Turners Hill **8** C4
Turriff **41** F3
Tutbury **18** D3
Tutshill **12** B5
Tuxford **24** D6
Twechar **31** H3
Tweedmouth **33** G3
Tweedsmuir **32** B4
Twyford *Hants* **7** F3
Twyford *W'ham* **13** H6
Twynholm **26** D3
Twyning **12** C3
Tyndrum **35** H3
Tynemouth **29** E2
Tythegston **11** F6
Tywardreath **3** H4
Tywyn **16** C5

U

Uachdar **44** B7
Uckfield **8** C4
Uddingston **31** H3
Uddington **32** A4
Uffculme **5** F3
Uig (Uige) **38** B2
Ulbster **43** H3
Ulceby **25** F4
Ulgham **28** D1
Ullapool (Ullapul) **39** F1
Ulleskelf **24** C2
Ulpha **27** G6
Ulsta **45** H2
Ulverston **22** B1
Umberleigh **4** D2
Unapool **42** B4
Undy **12** A5
Unstone **24** B6
Up Holland **22** D4
Upavon **7** E2
Uplyme **6** A5
Upper Clatford **7** F2
Upper Heyford **13** F3
Upper Knockando **40** C3
Upper Tean **18** C3
Uppingham **19** G5
Upton *ChesW&C* **22** C6
Upton *Dorset* **6** D5
Upton St. Leonards **12** C4
Upton upon Severn **12** C2
Urmston **23** E5
Ushaw Moor **28** D3
Usk **12** A4
Uttoxeter **18** C3
Uxbridge **14** A5
Uyeasound **45** J1

V

Valley **16** A2
Valsgarth **45** J1
Veensgarth **45** H4
Ventnor **7** G6
Verwood **6** D4
Vickerstown **22** B1
Vidlin **45** H3
Virginia Water **14** A6
Voe **45** H3

W

Waddesdon **13** H4
Waddington **25** E6
Wadebridge **3** H3
Wadhurst **8** D4
Wainfleet All Saints **20** B2
Wainhouse Corner **4** B4
Wakefield **24** B3
Walberswick **15** H1
Walderslade **15** E6

Wales **24** B5
Wallasey **22** B5
Wallingford **13** G5
Walls **45** G4
Wallsend **29** E2
Walmer **9** H3
Walsall **18** C5
Waltham **25** F4
Waltham Abbey **14** C4
Waltham on the
   Wolds **19** G3
Walthamstow **14** C5
Walton on the
   Naze **15** G3
Walton-le-Dale **22** D3
Walton-on-
   Thames **14** B6
Wandsworth **14** B6
Wantage **13** F5
Warboys **14** C1
Warcop **28** B5
Wardington **13** F2
Ware **14** C4
Wareham **6** D6
Wargrave **13** H6
Wark **28** B2
Warkworth **33** H5
Warlingham **8** C3
Warmington **13** F2
Warminster **6** C2
Warrington **22** D5
Warslow **18** C2
Warton **22** D1
Warwick **13** E1
Warwick Bridge **27** H3
Washingborough **25** E6
Washington **29** E3
Wass **24** C1
Watchet **5** F1
Watchgate **28** A6
Water Orton **18** D5
Waterbeach **14** C1
Waterbeck **27** G2
Waterlooville **7** G4
Watford **14** B5
Wath upon Dearne **24** B4
Watlington **13** G5
Watten **43** G3
Watton **21** E4
Watton-at-Stone **14** C4
Weaverham **22** D6
Wedmore **6** A2
Wednesbury **18** C5
Weedon Bec **13** F1
Weem **36** B2
Weisdale **45** H4
Weldon **19** H5
Wellesbourne **13** E2
Wellingborough **13** H1
Wellington *Som* **5** G2
Wellington *Tel&W* **18** A4
Wells **6** B2
Wells-next-the-Sea **21** E2
Welney **20** C5
Welshpool
   (Y Trallwng) **17** F5
Welton **25** E5
Welwyn **14** B4
Welwyn Garden
   City **14** B4
Wem **18** A3
Wembdon **5** G2
Wembley **14** B5
Wemyss Bay **31** F3
Wendens Ambo **14** D3
Wendover **13** H4
Wendron **3** F5
Wensley **28** C6
Wentworth **24** B5
Weobley **12** A2
Wereham **20** C4
West Auckland **28** D4
West Bergholt **15** F3

West Bridgford **19** F3
West Bromwich **18** C5
West Calder **32** B2
West Coker **6** B4
West Grinstead **8** B4
West Haddon **13** G1
West Harptree **6** B2
West Hill **5** F4
West Kilbride **31** F4
West Kirby **22** B5
West Knapton **24** D1
West Lavington **6** D2
West Linton **32** C3
West Lulworth **6** C5
West Malling **8** D3
West Meon **7** G3
West Mersea **15** F4
West Monkton **5** G2
West Moors **6** D4
West Sandwick **45** H2
West Somerton **21** G4
West Tarbert **30** D3
West Winch **20** C4
West Wycombe **13** H5
Westbury **6** C2
Westcott **8** B3
Westerdale **43** G3
Westergate **8** A5
Westerham **8** C3
Westfield **9** E5
Westgate **28** C4
Westhill **41** F5
Westleton **15** H1
Westnewton **27** G3
Weston *Dorset* **6** B6
Weston *Staffs* **18** C3
Weston-super-
  Mare **12** A4
Westonzoyland **6** A3
Westruther **33** E3
Westward Ho! **4** C2
Wetheral **27** H3
Wetherby **24** B2
Weybridge **14** A6
Weymouth **6** B6
Whaley Bridge **23** F5
Whalton **28** D1
Whaplode **20** B3
Whauphill **26** C3
Wheatley Hill **29** E4
Wheaton Aston **18** B4

Wheddon Cross **5** F2
Wherwell **7** F2
Whickham **28** D2
Whiddon Down **4** D4
Whimple **5** F4
Whiston **24** B5
Whitburn **32** B2
Whitby **29** G5
Whitchurch
  Bucks **13** H3
Whitchurch
  Cardiff **11** H6
Whitchurch *Hants* **7** F2
Whitchurch *Shrop* **18** A2
Whitecraig **32** D2
Whitehall **45** D2
Whitehaven **27** F5
Whitehill **7** H3
Whitehills **41** E2
Whiteness **45** H4
Whiterashes **41** F4
Whitfield **9** G3
Whithorn **26** C3
Whiting Bay **31** E5
Whitland **10** C4
Whitley Bay **29** E2
Whitnash **15** F1
Whitstable **15** G6
Whittingham **33** G5
Whittington **17** G4
Whittlesey **20** A5
Whitworth **23** E4
Wick *High* **43** H3
Wick *SGlos* **12** C6
Wick *VGlam* **11** G6
Wick *WSuss* **8** A5
Wickersley **24** B5
Wickford **15** E5
Wickham **7** G4
Wickham Market **15** G2
Wickwar **12** C5
Widecombe in the
  Moor **5** E5
Widford **14** C4
Widnes **22** D5
Wigan **22** D4
Wigmore **12** A1
Wigston **19** F5
Wigton **27** G3
Wigtown **26** C3
Willaston **22** C6

Willingdon **8** D5
Willingham **14** C1
Willington *Derbys* **18** D3
Willington *Dur* **28** D4
Williton **5** F1
Willoughby **25** G6
Wilmington **14** D6
Wilmslow **23** E5
Wilton **6** D3
Wimbledon **14** B6
Wimblington **20** B5
Wimborne Minster **6** D4
Wincanton **6** C3
Winchburgh **32** B2
Winchcombe **12** D3
Winchelsea **9** F5
Winchester **7** F3
Windermere **27** H6
Windsor **14** A6
Windygates **37** E4
Winford **12** B6
Wing **13** H3
Wingate **29** E4
Wingerworth **24** B6
Wingham **9** G3
Winkfield **14** A6
Winkleigh **4** D3
Winnersh **13** H6
Winscombe **6** A2
Winsford **22** D6
Winsley **12** C6
Winslow **13** H3
Winston **28** D5
Winterbourne **12** B5
Winterbourne
  Abbas **6** B5
Winterton **25** E4
Winton **28** B5
Winwick **20** A5
Wirksworth **18** D2
Wisbech **20** B4
Wishaw **32** A1
Wistanstow **17** G6
Wistaston **18** A2
Witham **15** E4
Witheridge **5** E3
Withernsea **25** G3
Witley **8** A4
Witney **13** F4
Wittering **19** H4
Witton Gilbert **28** D3

Wiveliscombe **5** F2
Wivenhoe **15** F3
Woburn **14** A3
Woburn Sands **14** A3
Woking **8** A3
Wokingham **13** H6
Wold Newton **25** E1
Wollaston **14** A1
Wolsingham **28** C4
Wolston **13** F1
Wolverhampton **18** C5
Wolverley **12** C1
Wolverton **13** H2
Wombourne **18** B5
Wombwell **24** B4
Wooburn **14** A5
Wood Green **14** B5
Woodborough **19** F2
Woodbridge **15** G2
Woodcote **13** G5
Woodhall Spa **25** F6
Woodingdean **8** C5
Woodland **28** C4
Woodley **13** H6
Woodmansey **25** E3
Woodplumpton **22** D3
Woodstock **13** F4
Woodton **21** F5
Woodville **19** E4
Wool **6** C5
Woolacombe **4** C1
Wooler **33** G4
Woolston **22** D5
Woolwich **14** C6
Wootton **14** A2
Wootton Bassett **12** D5
Worcester **12** C2
Worfield **18** B5
Workington **27** F4
Worksop **24** C6
Wormit **37** E3
Worplesdon **8** A3
Worth **8** C4
Worthing **8** B5
Wotton-under-
  Edge **12** C5
Woughton on the
  Green **13** H3
Wragby **25** F6
Wrangle **20** B2
Wrea Green **22** C3

Wrelton **29** G6
Wrexham
  (Wrecsam) **17** G3
Wrington **12** A6
Writtle **14** D4
Wroughton **13** E5
Wyberton **20** B2
Wye **9** F3
Wylye **6** D3
Wymondham
  Leics **19** G4
Wymondham
  Norf **21** F4
Wyre Piddle **12** D2
Wythall **12** D1

Y

Yapton **8** A5
Yarm **29** E5
Yarmouth **7** F5
Yarnton **13** F4
Yarrow **32** D4
Yate **12** C5
Yateley **13** H6
Yatton **12** A6
Yaxley **20** A5
Yeadon **24** A2
Yealmpton **4** D6
Yeovil **6** B4
Yeovilton **6** B3
Yetts o' Muckhart **36** C4
Ynysddu **11** H5
York **24** C2
Youlgreave **24** A6
Yoxall **18** D4
Yoxford **15** H1
Ysbyty Ystwyth **11** F1
Ystalyfera **11** F4
Ystrad **11** G5
Ystradgynlais **11** F4

Z

Zennor **3** E5